Roy!
Gre see
as always'
Chris

GUARDIANS OF THE GRAIL

OTHER BOOKS BY CHRISTOPHER DATTA

Touched with Fire
Fire and Dust
The Demon Stone

GUARDIANS OF THE GRAIL

A LIFE OF DIPLOMACY ON THE EDGE

CHRISTOPHER DATTA

ISBN-13: 978-1717500618
ISBN-10: 1717500617

Dedicated to Harold and Betty Datta
My Father and Mother

FOREWORD

I wrote this book to give people a look into what American Foreign Service Officers do and the risks we often take in the service of our country at embassies around the world. People are familiar with the sacrifices our men and women in uniform make, but often view diplomats as pinstriped scaredy-cats. However, since World War II more ambassadors have been killed in the line of duty than generals, and we are a much smaller force. We are the first line of defense when it comes to protecting our national interests, and often find ourselves in harm's way the same as our military colleagues.

This book is the arc of my Foreign Service career. As I became more senior, I was challenged with more difficult situations. How do we handle development work better? How do we promote democratic development without killing people? How do we keep America safe? How do we keep the peace without the use of force?

I want readers to come away with a better understanding of the value of diplomacy, an appreciation for the risks diplomats take, the complexity of the world we face, how much American diplomacy has done to make the world a better place, and where and how we have succeeded and, yes, how we have failed.

Special thanks to some of my early readers for their valuable contributions to this book, including Ambassador Thomas Krajeski, Ambassador John Blaney, my agents Jessica Papin and Sharon Pelletier and, most of all, to my wife, Debra Datta. Thanks also to Tracey Attlee, my portrait photographer, and Mallory Rock, the graphic designer for all my books.

CHAPTER 1

I was raised in a functional family by parents who loved me. It's a terrible burden for a writer not to have had a childhood of soul-rending despair from which to draw inspiration, as so many have. I wasn't beaten. My father wasn't an alcoholic wife-abuser. My siblings and cousins were and are friends. Sure, Mom and Dad weren't rich and didn't give me a fortune with which to buy a real-estate empire, like some. They did let me down there. But, basically, I didn't want for anything, which was thoughtless of them.

Well, there was the case of my grandfather, who was always kind to me but was a son of a bitch to my father growing up. Dad had plenty of reasons for being a great novelist, but he wasted that torment in raising a happy family of his own.

When my Grandmother Datta died, I remember how Grandfather collapsed at her coffin during the funeral, crying out, "How could you do this to me?"

I thought it odd that he would wail about her abandoning him. It's not as if she had a heart attack to spite him. Of course, it was true he had no idea how to get along on his own, having been waited on hand and foot his whole adult life, so I suppose it was understandable he was put out by her uncharitable departure.

I am reminded of the movie *My Big Fat Greek Wedding*, in which a woman from a loud and intrusive Greek family tells her boyfriend, who is an only child, "You don't understand what it's like. I have twenty first cousins."

Well, the Greeks have nothing over the Poles in Winona, Minnesota, where my family is from. I have twenty-five first cousins. And we, too, are loud and intrusive.

We are an extended family of many traditions. Picnics, family reunions, community service and more. My parents embodied all of those traditions. In July of 2017 we had a family reunion at Lake Winona, the scene of many family get-togethers over the decades. Fifty of us came, and that wasn't the whole family.

One bittersweet tradition of our family is to hold what we call a Polish Wake to honor the passing of one of our own. They are usually held at the home of my cousins, Scott and Kathy Turner. When my mother and uncle Bob, my dad's brother, passed in the same week, we had one to remember them. As we always do, we took turns exchanging memories and stories of the deceased. Some drinking was involved, I'll admit. The stories were happy and sad, often hilarious, and sometimes brutally honest. It's a great tradition because it is not a mourning, although tears are shed, but a celebration. A celebration of the life that has passed, of the gifts given to us by the those who have gone, and of the love we feel for each other. My only regret is that we have held so many of them of late.

My mother was one of the greatest, kindest souls I have ever known, and I'll just share one memory of her. When I was seventeen, I stayed out until 3:00 A.M. with my friends one Saturday night. My bedroom was in the basement, accessed by a side door that led downstairs to the basement and also up to the kitchen. I quietly unlocked the door and thought they would never know what time I'd come back. Then I heard heavy footsteps coming down the second-floor stairs. I walked up to the kitchen and my mother burst in, angry as a wet hen.

"How could you!? We were so worried. How dare you treat us like this?"

I knew I was busted and there was no recourse but to throw myself on the mercy of the court.

"You're right. I'm a terrible son. I don't know why you put up with it. You deserve so much better and I'm a disgrace to the family. If you were to shoot me right now, God himself would call it justice. I have no excuse and you should beat me mercilessly."

As I'm saying this, the corners of her mouth start to twitch up. She really wanted to be mad but was starting to laugh and couldn't help it. Finally, she burst out, "Oh, shut up and go to bed!"

I never did it again. At least, not that she knew of.

My dad grew up in the Great Depression and, like many of his generation, it had a lasting impact on his view of life and financial insecurity. He was generous with everyone except himself, never gambled, sold any stock he had the minute it went up, brooded incessantly when one went down and he was obsessively afraid to spend money. He once walked out of a restaurant because they didn't have a lunch menu, even though I was paying.

He did buy long-term care insurance because he never wanted to be a burden to his family. He originally purchased a policy that lasted as long as he did, but then discovered it was cheaper to get the two-year limit variety and switched to that. He developed Parkinson's and did have to go to a nursing home. He died on July 10, 2014 at age eighty-eight. His long-term care insurance was set to expire the following month. That was Dad. Five thousand dollars a month for nursing-home care? No way was he going to pay that himself. Goodbye. Thanks for the memories. One of the last things he said was, "It sure went by fast." It sure does.

I grew up reading comic books, and my favorite hero was Green Lantern. In fact, I early on memorized the Green Lantern pledge he recited to recharge the ring that gave him his superhero powers. I liked Green Lantern best because he was just an ordinary guy until a dying spaceman gave him a Green Lantern ring. He was not born to power, like Superman. I liked Batman, but even at seven years of age I knew what Batman did was simply not humanly possible. Spiderman was good, but where was I going to find a radioactive spider to give me spider powers? Besides, I have arachnophobia.

But what if there are aliens? It's a big universe with plenty of room. And if they can cruise the galaxy, it stands to reason they would posses amazing technology beyond our grasp, including power rings. And just maybe one of them would think I merited such a ring to defend humanity from evil. Sure, it was a one-in-a-billion shot, but millions of people buy lottery tickets, and the odds on any one of them winning are about the same as me becoming a Green Lantern. Sadly, I never got that power ring, and I haven't won the lottery, either.

Dad's fear of financial insecurity made him a nuisance when I reached my twenties. At the time, he worked for the United States Agency for International Development, or USAID, our international aid program, and he was stationed in Washington, DC. An early riser all his life, he got to the office at 6:00 A.M. his time, which was 5:00 A.M. in Minneapolis where I lived. At least three times a week he called me at 5:00 A.M. to ask if I was going to be a bum *all* my life. The problem was, he just would not take "Yes" for an answer. My only regret about my party-boy twenties is that I can't go back and do it all over again.

So to stop the calls I signed up to take the Foreign Service Officer exam for the United States Information Agency. This was made easier by the fact that Dad kept sending me applications. He even sent me postage for the envelope.

This was a curious thing for him to do because he disliked his job at USAID. It was not that he did not believe in helping poor people in other countries to better their lives; he disliked his job precisely *because* he believed in helping poor people in other countries to better their lives. Economic development for poor nations is a complicated and long-term undertaking, but Congress is poor at understanding anything complicated, and it has the patience of a three-year-old on a sugar rush. When Congress gave USAID money, ten days later they wanted to know what the results were. On top of that, during the Cold War they mandated that many USAID development programs be used as personal checking accounts for all manner of despotic tyrants who sided with us against the Communists. And then, like the police inspector in the movie *Casablanca* who is shocked to learn there is gambling going on in the casino where he is gambling, Congress was shocked to learn that their money had been wasted. Since they could not tell voters it was their doing, something had to be wrong at USAID, and the solution was more micro-managing to see to it that the money for foreign development was being spent in someone's home district to buy tractors or cars or road equipment that was not needed and could be purchased more cheaply elsewhere.

Be that as it may, if applying to the Foreign Service would get my Dad off my back at 5:00 A.M., I was happy to comply. However, it was a textbook example of a tactical success and a strategic failure: a tactical success because I got my Dad to stop his early morning calls, but a strategic failure because a year and a half later I got the job.

So, instead of getting a Green Lantern power ring, I joined the United States Department of State in the hope that by being in the diplomatic corps of the best country on Earth I could still work some good in the world. Being a superhero would, of course, have been better, but I settled for what I could get.

But I do still buy the occasional lottery ticket, and I look up at the stars at night, waiting.

CHAPTER 2

When I was offered a job in the Foreign Service, my Grandmother Helga Rehn was ecstatic.

She had come to the United States from Sweden by herself at age nineteen and, as you might expect, she was strong and fearless. It was often my job to chauffeur her to family events. I drove an old puke-beige Ford Fairlane that I maintained myself because I could not afford to take it to a garage. It ran well, but in Minnesota the streets are treated with salt in the winter, which is hell on car bodies. Mine was so rusted you could see the road passing by through holes in the floor, and the only way to keep the car doors shut was to tie them closed with rope. That didn't faze Helga. On the other hand, she refused to ride my motorcycle. She said she'd split in half if she tried. When I lived in Minnesota, we had dinner together in her apartment nearly every Sunday evening.

Helga lived to 104.

My Grandfather Rehn, on the other hand, was a severe alcoholic and died when I was quite young. It was Helga who worked and held the family together. She didn't have much, but what she did, she made go a long way.

For some reason, she always believed in me, and as a going-away present she gave me my first briefcase, a Samsonite hard shell. She thought it made me look professional. I carried it to Washington and used it for many years.

I joined the State Department shortly after President Ronald Reagan was inaugurated, and one of his first acts was to place a hiring freeze on all government agencies. My Foreign Service class was the very first exemption to that freeze. Ronald Reagan granted a waiver because he believed in the power and importance of diplomacy, and he later appointed George Shultz Secretary of State, one of the most talented men to ever hold that office.

There were fourteen of us in my class, and we spent a year as junior officers learning diplomatic tradecraft and studying a foreign language. Knowing a second language is a requirement to be tenured as a Foreign Service Officer, and you have four years to acquire one, or you're out. I studied French, but a few years later had to take on Arabic for an assignment to Jordan.

The illogical nature of languages is stunning. Just talk to someone learning English to get an earful about how nonsensical ours is.

Words that sound the same often have subtle pronunciation distinctions that make a big difference to a native speaker. In a restaurant, when asked what tip to leave, I once advised the person in French to leave the waiter his infant son when I had meant to say one French franc. Another time, instead of asking the waiter for the bill, I requested breakfast. I had just finished dinner.

In French, certain verbs are reflexive, like the verb "to remember." You say, literally, "I remember myself going to the store."

I figured if "to remember" is reflexive, then "to forget" must be, too. So I constructed a sentence making "to forget" reflexive, and my teacher fell over laughing.

That was a better reaction than when she got a glassy and suspicious look, indicating that I had somehow managed to proposition her.

By making "to forget" reflexive, I said that I "had forgot myself," which means in French I soiled my pants.

I know another fellow who spoke fluent French that he learned in Africa, where in French you commonly refer to children as "eggs." He went to French-speaking Canada for a visit and was having a pleasant conversation with a cabbie when he asked him how many "eggs" he had.

The cab driver grew sullen and cold. When asked why, the cabbie finally answered, "Well, I have two, not that it's any of your business."

My friend answered, "My grandfather had eight."

That set the driver off into gales of laughter, during which he repeated between gasps, "Eight? Eight?"

Turns out that in French-speaking Canada, my friend had asked the cabbie how many testicles he had.

So, a little bit of knowledge can be a dangerous thing when it comes to languages, especially when you're a diplomat. Two classic cases are President Kennedy and President Carter.

When Kennedy went to Berlin, he did not really say in German, "I am a Berliner." What he actually said was, "I am a cream-filled pastry." People cheered anyway because they knew what he meant, or maybe they were hungry.

And when President Carter went to Poland and in a speech said he was "fond" of the Polish people, his interpreter, who had not lived in Poland in many years, used the verb meaning he was "sexually attracted" to the Polish people. I am sure his audience thought, "First Russia screwed us, now the U.S. wants a turn."

Many years later I was assigned to Senegal. In the native language of Wolof, the name Datta, if pronounced with a soft "a", means vagina. I had to change it to Datta with a hard "a" to avoid being addressed as Mr. Vagina, which would have made it hard to be taken seriously in polite conversation. The hard "a" was like the difference between Regina and vagina.

You may be the equivalent of William Shakespeare in English, but when you start Arabic, a five-year-old in a Cairo shantytown sounds better educated.

Memorizing vocabulary is tough. To speak a language fluently, you need to know around 10,000 words. To push my retention to the limit, I did develop a technique I'll share with you.

Get yourself a stack of index cards, a pencil and tape. Write the new word you want to memorize in pencil on the index card and tape the card to a wall at eye level. Stare at the word for thirty seconds and then start hitting the word with your forehead. When there is blood on the card, you are pretty certain to remember it. Brick walls provide better memory retention than sheetrock.

But I passed my French exam in time for my first overseas assignment to Madras in South India.

CHAPTER 3

During my first diplomatic assignment to South India, the luxury passenger ship *Queen Elizabeth 2* came to port. The ship contacted us because they had a dead American on board they needed sent home. That is a service an American embassy will perform for you. Alive or dead, we'll get you home.

When I got to the dock, it was packed with bicycle rickshaw drivers looking for fares. Their vehicles are like the rickshaws in the movies set in China, except the cart is attached to a bicycle the owner peddles instead of being on foot. In India, these vehicles are elaborately decorated with colorful paintings of trees, flowers, animals and Hindu gods.

The reason there were so many at the port was that a few years earlier a visiting American couple had disembarked from the *QE2* and rode around town in one. They fell in love with it and decided it would make a terrific garden ornament back home, so they asked the fellow how much he wanted for it. He said two thousand, and they gave him $2,000. He had meant 2,000 rupees, which was about the equivalent of $200. Two thousand dollars was more than this guy would earn in a lifetime of backbreaking work.

Word got around, and now every rickshaw driver in town met the *QE2* hoping to take on another dream tourist.

The *QE2* is an impressive floating city. It has electrical power plants, stores, bars, medical facilities, apartments, sanitation, dining facilities, telecommunications, administrative services, casinos, nightclubs and, of course, a morgue.

Well, not of course. It surprised me that a floating luxury palace had a refrigerated facility for storing corpses.

I learned quite a few people die on these trips. It is not that sailing on the QE2 is inherently unhealthy; it is just that your average passenger is elderly, and some are downright ancient.

My decedent, Ruby, was in her mid-eighties and had quietly passed away at sea of a heart attack. I suppose she knew this trip was one of the last she would take, and thought she should see something of the planet while she still could, a kind of Bilbo Baggins on an adventure.

And see the world she did; at least, about half of it. She died just before reaching Sri Lanka, the halfway point on her trip. The QE2 staff wanted to bury her at sea, which is an option when you die on a luxury cruise, but her family back in Ohio wanted her home.

There are many regulations for shipping bodies internationally. For instance, they have to be embalmed. Simple enough, except that Hindus are cremated, so there were not many embalming facilities in South India. After a great deal of searching, we finally found one and they agreed to send a hearse to pick up Ruby at the dock.

My first stop on the ship was at the medical officer's desk to pick up Ruby's paperwork and her death certificate, duly signed by the captain. It was here I received my first piece of bad news. When the ship stopped briefly in Sri Lanka, the American embassy there had come to get the details concerning Ruby's death and then ask the family whether they wanted burial at sea or for us to send her home.

The ship left before the request to send the body home arrived. The problem was, the embassy had taken Ruby's passport. Now you might think a dead person does not need a passport, but you would be wrong.

Our next stop was to see the Indian customs and immigration agents who had a temporary office next to the ship to facilitate tourists visiting (and spending money) for the day.

We explained that Ruby would be disembarking, and they asked for her passport. I explained that she was dead and had unfortunately lost her passport, and they insisted that Ruby could not leave the ship without one. I promised that Ruby would not steal anything, deal drugs, engage in any kind of gang activity, start a prostitution ring, throw wild parties or in any other way make a nuisance of herself.

They were unconvinced.

We argued, and they finally agreed that it was up to their supervisor to make an exception, if an exception could be made.

Fine, I answered, where could I find their supervisor?

He was on the ship and they did not know where.

When I asked one of the British officers where I could find him, he hemmed and hawed and finally explained that to help ease the way for passengers to get through customs for the day, the customs supervisor had been given free run of the ship. There were in excess of twenty bars on the QE2, and this fellow was apparently making a determined effort to visit each and every one, drinks on the house.

In South India it was possible to drink, but to do so required a doctor's certificate certifying you to be an incurable alcoholic who would die if you did not get your daily fix. Doctors willing to issue such certificates were in hot demand, and there were those who did nothing else. Doctors of mixology, as it were.

I, as an American diplomat, was automatically issued a certificate stating I was an incurable drunk because I was an American, and everyone in India knew from the movies that all Americans are incurable drunks.

Touring the bars on the QE2 drinking the best liquor money could buy at no cost was a real treat for this customs agent, and in exchange the passengers of the QE2 were certainly getting the red carpet treatment from his staff on the dock; except for poor Ruby, of course, who was in a fix.

About this time, the hearse arrived with the crew from the funeral parlor. I had to admit, they were making an effort to look the part of professional undertakers, even if they did not quite pull it off.

The hearse was a very, very old Ford station wagon, the kind with wood-paneled sides. I cannot remember the last time I saw one of those. The wood was peeling off in large pieces, but the car had been painted black, a real concession in this extremely hot climate. And they had brought a coffin and men to carry it. They had, however, forgotten to bring the coffin lid.

The laborers were needed because the Hindu caste system is strict about a number of things, including the handling of the dead. Only casteless people, also known as "untouchables," can touch the dead. It would be spiritually polluting for anyone else to do it.

So now I had my car, my coffin and the guys I needed to carry Ruby off the ship. If I could find the customs supervisor to authorize Ruby's departure, I was set. To move things along, we carried the coffin up the gangplank into the ship, transferred Ruby's frozen body to it, and placed her in a side corridor discreetly out of view so she was ready to go as soon as we received permission.

We waited. The supervisor did not show.

Finally, a nervous British officer pulled me aside to say that they needed us to get Ruby off the ship. The problem, he said, was that a very wealthy maharaja from Malaysia would soon be boarding with his extensive entourage. He had reserved some very expensive suites, and he could be counted upon to lose a handsome sum in the casino. The management of the ship wanted to ensure nothing would happen that might cause him to cancel this trip.

If Ruby were coming down the gangway as he was coming up, he would certainly see it as an omen of doom, and would never set foot on the ship.

I explained the situation with Ruby's passport, but he insisted that Ruby should leave as soon as possible. She could wait in the car until her paperwork was in order, so long as there was no coffin in sight.

After studying the situation, I collected the pallbearers, had them shoulder the coffin and started them down to the dock. When the customs men realized what was happening, they immediately ran up waving their arms and shouting that Ruby was not allowed to disembark.

This made the pallbearers jumpy and two of them slipped. The lidless coffin careened to the side, and Ruby fell halfway out, balanced precariously on the coffin's edge, which was hanging over the water.

It looked as if Ruby was going to be buried at sea, after all. Well, I thought, this could be a really short career. I was already composing in my mind the letter I would have to write to the family, along the lines of, "Ruby, I am sorry to say, wanted to be buried at sea and took matters into her own hands by jumping into the Bay of Bengal. I hope you understand. It was not my fault. As we all know, she was a strong-willed woman who did what she damn well pleased to the very end."

The good news was that the harbor was so filthy, another body bobbing around would hardly attract attention.

It was a close call, but the guys recovered their balance, righted themselves, and Ruby disappeared back into her box. We continued down the gangplank, the customs men having a cow, but I was counting on their not being willing to come closer than about fifteen feet to that dead body for fear of spiritually polluting themselves.

I was right. As we advanced, they backed off and we got Ruby into the station wagon where we covered her up, to the relief of the British crew. I then explained to the irate customs men that Ruby was not going anywhere, we just needed to get her into the car, and I promised them that she had agreed to wait there patiently until their supervisor arrived.

That grudgingly satisfied them, and we once again waited.

I was looking through the papers concerning Ruby, which included all the medical reports from the ship's surgeon signed by him and the captain, when I had an idea.

Indians love paperwork, almost to the point of a religion. They learned it from the British when they were a part of the Empire. When you go into a department store to buy something, you bring the object you want to a check-in counter where it is taken from you and you are given a ticket. You take the ticket to a cash register where you pay for the item and are issued a receipt. You take that receipt to a third counter, where another clerk waits for the delivery of the item, and when he finally receives it, he takes your ticket and hands you the package. It is a kind of dance, and all the way along your dance ticket has to be stamped and punched multiple times by the proper person.

I asked the ship's purser if he could make copies of the papers I had, and he complied.

Not long after, our wandering Customs Supervisor staggered off the ship, drunk as a skunk and looking it. His men gathered around him with me, everyone talking at once about the situation, with lots of exclamations on the part of the lower-ranked men about "No proper documentation. None at all."

The supervisor eyed the hearse balefully and then looked to me. "She has no passport, you are saying?"

"Yes," I answered, "it was taken in Colombo when the ship stopped in Sri Lanka."

"So why were they not taking the body?"

"They were waiting for word from the family on what to do with her, and it came too late."

"But now she has no passport."

"She is dead," I said.

He shook his head mournfully. "It is not mattering. There must be the proper signing."

And this is where I first exhibited my fine grasp of the art of diplomacy that has so distinguished my career. "Ah," I said, "but I have the proper signing," waving one of the medical reports. "This document here conclusively records that Ruby Disseldorf is dead."

It was like I was the Munchkin doctor in *The Wizard of Oz* certifying the demise of the Wicked Witch.

"Look," I said, pointing to a section of the death certificate.

"But does it have the proper signing?" he asked, intrigued but suspicious.

"Absolutely," I answered. "The doctor, as you can see, signed it here. *And* the captain of the ship has signed it on the second page."

"The captain has signed it?" he said, searching for the signature. Finding it, he smiled. "Yes," he said, "I think this will do."

The rest of the customs men looked crestfallen. "But we need copies," they objected.

"Not a problem," I said, and I passed papers all around, a copy for everyone. It was a happy fizzy party, and with everyone placated, they signed our release papers and I finally bid a fond farewell to Ruby as the old station wagon trundled away.

I am happy to say that we finally did get Ruby home, where she rests to this day, the most traveled corpse in the cemetery. Her family did not want her personal effects sent home. It would, they thought, cost more than it was worth to get them. So we held an auction.

Ruby had purchased many little souvenirs along the way, including scarves, a few necklaces and other items that were not particularly expensive. Our Consular Officer, Tom Krajeski, sold them all and donated the money to a local charity. I think Ruby would have liked that, and, given her attempt to jump into the Bay of Bengal, I would also bet that she would have preferred to be buried at sea, where she would have been reincarnated as a mermaid.

CHAPTER 4

After India I went to staff the Public Diplomacy office at our embassy in Jordan, a large operation compared with most other embassies, and it included a Public Affairs Officer in charge of all Public Diplomacy operations, a Cultural Affairs Officer and, my job, the Information Center Director.

I ran our library, our film program, published a monthly newsletter and created an annual schedule of cultural events, among other things. You could say I was an impresario. It was great fun, except for the terrorism that was then beginning to erupt in the region.

While I was in Jordan, the Soviet Union tried to recruit me to spy for them.

A Soviet Lt. Colonel in the KGB—I will call him Ivan although I actually no longer remember his name—came to the American Cultural Center to introduce himself. He was active in, he said, the Soviet Cultural Center, which was just down the street from ours. After I showed him around my operation, he asked if I would like to see his.

Ivan was a nice guy. Young, articulate and with a twinkle in his eye that said, "You know what I'm about," meaning, how would you like to come work for us? I did know what was up, of course, but told him I would like to see his center. I would call and arrange a time.

Before I could set a time, I was required to speak to our political office at the embassy to get their permission. In those days you could not meet with the Russians without reporting it, unless, of course, you actually did intend to spy for them. If discovered, meeting with Russians and not reporting it would lose me my security clearance and my job. That seems to be not so true in the current Administration.

I was given the embassy's blessing to go see Ivan.

He sounded a little surprised to hear back from me. I suppose he thought I was just being polite when I said I would come. He probably thought my embassy would not let me, but he knew one of two things. Either I had gone to the embassy and they had given me permission to visit, or I was willing to talk to them on my own about becoming a spy.

We set the appointment for 9:00 A.M. on a Thursday morning. Since their office was close, I walked. It also played into the game, of course, because if I had taken an embassy car, that would have announced that the embassy knew where I was.

Ivan greeted me at the front door with a warm smile and firm handshake. We quickly walked through the Soviet Cultural Center, passing tables where Jordanian patrons were playing chess (we did not have board games at my center), and I was led to a back room office where I was invited to sit.

Ivan disappeared for a few minutes and I was seemingly left by myself. I am sure hidden camera eyes watched me to see what I would do left on my own. Plant a bug, perhaps, or look though the papers on the desk.

I was not up to anything except curiosity, so I sat and waited patiently until Ivan finally returned with a colleague. He introduced me and we sat down to some chitchat. How did I like their center? Where was I from? And, oh, would I ever like to visit the Soviet Union? I could, I was told, take some spectacular trips by car, which they could arrange if I wanted to go.

I allowed that I had never seen Mother Russia and it would be interesting to take a trip. About that time, a Jordanian came in with a bottle of Johnny Walker Black Label scotch and glasses. Ivan poured healthy shots all around.

This was about 9:30 in the morning, but if I had to sacrifice my liver for the good of my country, then I was going to do it. We drank. And then we drank some more.

A good friend of mine (an academic) who spent a few years in Russia later told me there was nothing exceptional about this. The Russians always drink, and he had never spent as much time intoxicated as he did when he lived there. He said he could never figure out how they ever got anything done. That they had been a superpower for as long as they were amazed him.

So Ivan and I drank scotch and talked at length about the wonders of the Soviet Union that I could see by car, if I chose to go. In the middle of this, an older hawk-faced man stepped into the room and stared at me for several minutes without saying a word. Ivan glanced at him and continued our conversation. When the stranger satisfied himself with whatever he had come to see, he left as silently as he had appeared.

I later learned from our own people that he was the head of KGB operations in Jordan.

As I was getting really looped, Ivan suggested we continue with the tour of his center, which was fine by me. By that time, just about anything was fine by me. This was certainly different from how my day at work normally started.

I saw the library and the lecture hall and all the usual facilities one has at a cultural center. It was not all that different in layout from my own. I did find one rack of pamphlets in English dealing with such subjects as "CIA Terrorism Around the World," "How America Corrupts Youth," "The American Plan for World Domination" and "America and the Zionist Plot for the Middle East." This was great stuff and I wanted it all. They gave me a copy of each.

After we had a good look around, Ivan offered to drive me back. I could have walked, really, but things were reeling so I accepted his offer.

As we pulled up in front of my building, we looked at each other. We both smiled.

"Do you want to work for us?" he said.

"No," I answered. "How about you? Want to work for us?"

He just smiled back.

I thanked him for a most interesting morning, and got out of the car.

A few times I invited Ivan over to my house for dinner. He sounded interested and told me he would have to check his schedule and get back to me. As it turned out, his dance card was always full. That is, his boss was more afraid I would turn Ivan than that he would turn me.

It was too bad. I would have liked to know him better. His boss gave me the willies, but I liked Ivan.

After I left Jordan, I never heard from him or any other Soviet agent again. I guess they gave up on me.

CHAPTER 5

Once every two weeks, the American embassy in Jordan sent a courier to our consulate in Jerusalem to exchange mail and official correspondence, including classified reports. The round trip was made by car. If not for the border between Jordan and Israel, the drive to Jerusalem would take just two or three hours.

The opportunity to make the trip was given on a rotating basis to all the American officers in the embassy with a security clearance.

My turn came around and I was given instructions on how the process worked, what was expected of me, and where I was to go. My father-in-law was visiting at the time, and I was given permission to take him along.

Wes was a big fellow, tall and white-haired. He was excited to be on an official courier mission delivering secret correspondence. I did not have the heart to tell him that the U.S.G. over-classifies most everything, and I doubted we carried anything you could not learn by reading the *New York Times*. I once saw a classified cable, for instance, whose sole subject was an Internet website that anyone could view on the World Wide Web.

The military is even worse. I once got a cable from them listing talking points to be used with journalists concerning an overseas training program, and the talking points were classified "confidential," which meant I could not reveal them to anyone who did not possess a government clearance. I don't know of any journalists with such a clearance.

The drive from Amman to the Israeli border takes only forty minutes. We first had to check through Jordanian border control, which was somewhat ironic given that Jordan did not recognize Israel and considered the land on the opposite side of the Jordan River to be its own, which it was before the 1967 war. The Jordan River defined their unrecognized border, and the single-lane iron bridge with a wooden floor across the river was usually called the Allenby Bridge, although it was also known as the King Hussein Bridge.

A Jordanian soldier marked my passport, but did not stamp it, since as far as he was concerned I was not actually leaving Jordan.

Border procedures took about a half hour on the Jordanian side. When completed, we drove on to the bridge.

I know the old folk song says, "The Jordan River is deep and wide," but it is not. It's shallow and not more than about fifty feet wide. It is also green, thanks to the wonders of pollution and agricultural runoff. Or at least it was back in 1985 when I last crossed it.

On the Jordanian side, I remember there being a large white house, covered in sandbags and swarming with heavily armed troops all staring intently and with some show of menace at the Israeli soldiers similarly situated and easily visible on the other side of this narrow river.

The routine was to drive the embassy car halfway across the bridge and stop, square in the middle of these two heavily armed camps with nothing to do all day but stare daggers at each other and, in this case, stare daggers at me.

The reason I had to stop was to change license plates before entering Israel. I had Jordanian plates, but could not change to Israeli plates in Jordan. I also could not enter Israel with Jordanian plates, so I was required to stop in the middle of the river in no man's land.

I opened the trunk where the Israeli plates were stored, along with a screwdriver to remove the bolts holding the plates on the car.

I replaced the Jordanian plates with Israeli plates, put the Jordanian ones in the trunk along with the screwdriver, and Wes and I continued on our way. We did, that is, until stopped by a heavily armed Israeli soldier who inspected the car and then waved us through to the Israeli border processing station.

On the Israeli side the procedures were similar to what we had gone through in Jordan, although the buildings were more modern.

Except that in the case of the Israelis, they *wanted* to stamp my passport to show that I had entered Israel. This had the potential to cause me grief because I traveled widely in the region, and most Arab countries would turn me away if they found an Israeli stamp in my passport. For that reason, I carried two diplomatic passports, one for travel to Israel and one for the rest of the world.

The drive to Jerusalem from the Allenby Bridge takes you through Jericho in the Jordan River Valley, where the walls came a-tumbling down, and up through some of the most desolate land you will ever see. The valley itself is fairly green because of irrigation, but as you climb out of the valley, the landscape is a moonscape. Yet this is some of the most fought-over land in the history of humanity.

After dropping off the diplomatic pouch at the American consulate in Jerusalem, Wes and I continued on to the American Colony Hotel, just outside the old city of Jerusalem. It is one of the great hotels of that city, originally built in the mid-1800s by a rich Arab landowner for himself and his four wives, and later bought by American investors who transformed it into a hotel. T.E. Lawrence, I am told, often stayed there. It's the kind of place where ghosts and spies meet.

Wes and I spent a couple of days exploring Jerusalem. In those days, it was a happier city. There were still tensions between the Jewish and Arab inhabitants, god knows, but they mostly got along better, in a live-and-let-live way. The old city is a classic ancient town, a bewildering maze of narrow stone streets running through dim canyons of gray stone shops and houses.

Wes was religious, and wanted to visit the Church of the Holy Sepulcher. It is an impressive church, and is symbolic of the whole city.

First of all, it is the source of chronic conflict, even (or in this case especially) among Christians. It is reputed to encompass both the places of Jesus's crucifixion and burial. I've seen reports that say this is simply improbable, while others disagree. Your choice.

Several Christian sects own various pieces of the church. Possession was arrived at after a great deal of sometimes violent dispute. Roman Catholics, Copts, Ethiopian Orthodox, and others all now share a joint ownership which dictates who can do what and where in the church, from sweeping the floors to holding ceremonies. The rivalry was so intense at one point that no one could decide who should hold the key to lock and unlock the front door.

The entrance is called Omar's door, named after the first Muslim leader to capture Jerusalem from the Christians. He refused to convert the church to a mosque, and allowed freedom of religion to all inhabitants of the city, unlike the Crusaders who just killed or forcibly converted non-Christians. The only way this highly prized privilege could be managed without bloodshed was for the key to be given to a Muslim family who had no dog in the fight, so to speak. The key has stayed in this family for generations, and only a member of the family can lock and unlock the church door.

It was a great solution.

But that, most assuredly, is Jerusalem, a city of competing interests concerning things that would leave an alien just landed on Earth scratching whatever passed for its head regarding the seemingly meaningless issues we are regularly willing to kill each other over with horrific violence and in great numbers.

There are two special places in the Church of the Holy Sepulcher, one being the purported site of the crucifixion, and the other where Jesus is said to have been interred.

Wes and I first went to the burial site. Over the centuries this was a place for the worship of pagan deities before there were Christians. At one point, a Muslim ruler had the whole Christian shrine torn down, and he had stonemasons quarry out all of the hill down to the bare rock base, intending to eliminate any possibility of re-establishing it as a Christian place of worship.

Foolish man.

Today, a rather odd box-like structure stands inside the church on the spot where it is believed Jesus was interred, which you enter to stand in the holy site and which is lit by candles and oil lamps.

Next, we went to the place of the crucifixion, not far away.

A rock juts up from the floor, surrounded by altars and other holy icons. We stood in line and eventually found ourselves at the summit standing before a hole in the rock where, we were told, the cross had been anchored. We were permitted to place a hand in the hole. It felt odd to me, sticking my hand down into a dark hole, having not the slightest idea what might be in it. I could not help but worry it might be a Stephen King moment, with something grabbing and dragging me down to my doom.

When we finished, we noticed another line of pilgrims about twenty feet away, also kneeling and touching the floor.

When we inquired why, we were told that another Christian sect was sure that this was the actual location where Jesus's cross had stood, not the place where we were.

I visualized a neon sign: "Been to the site of the crucifixion? Now come to the real thing instead of that cheap fake rat-infested hole you just stuck your hand in." You can also buy a "genuine fake" piece of the true cross. All the surrounding shops sold them.

I have lived in India and seen the spectacle of thousands of Hindus praying to gods that send shivers down the spines of many Christians. I have lived in Buddhist countries where the search for enlightenment is the way to nirvana. I have lived in Africa and met people who thought that god was in the streams and rocks and trees. I have lived in the Middle East and watched orthodox Jews in black coats and beards running across Jerusalem to get home on a Friday before sunset and the beginning of the Sabbath. And I have lain awake at night in Muslim lands listening to the muezzin calling to god from the minaret of a local mosque. There are so many paths to god, what does it matter if the true cross was in one hole in a rock or in another one fifteen feet away, or nowhere near there at all?

All too often, not only does it mean a lot, but the overwhelming majority of people, as an article of "faith" (which is to say that they believe it for the simple reason that they *want* to believe it), must feel that what they believe is the only way to believe, and it keeps them awake at night to imagine that there are people in this world who think they are wrong. Their faith is not sufficient to make them happy until they can make others see things as they do, or kill them for not seeing, as if god would really want you to murder in god's name.

When I was a kid, I used to watch a TV quiz show called *To Tell the Truth*, in which a panel of four people tried to correctly identify which of three contestants posing as the same noteworthy person was actually him or her. At the end of the show, the master of ceremonies asked the real person to stand up. The contestants won money based on how many of the panelists the imposters were able to fool.

I feel like I'm playing that game whenever I meet a painfully concerned Christian fundamentalist who asks me, "Do you know Jesus and accept Him as your savior?"

There are more manifestations of Jesus worshipped today than there are Hindu gods. It is beyond me why anyone calls Christianity a monotheistic religion.

If you answered in the affirmative to the Jesus question and then said you were a Mormon, most conservative Baptists would hold their fingers up in a cross and shout, "Get thee behind me, Satan!"

Pope John Paul II once issued an edict clarifying that if you don't kneel down to the Jesus of the Roman Catholic Church, you are barking up the wrong tree and you can forget about heaven because you ain't a-going there. Most evangelicals return that favor to Roman Catholics, confidently predicting their slow roast in hell for worshiping a false god.

Seventh Day Adventists, Jehovah's Witnesses, Baptists, Calvinists and so on and so forth all know they have the inside track on the real Jesus, and boiling in oil is too good for all the rest of you deluded heretics. In past centuries, and even today in many places, praying to the wrong Jesus can get you put to death by folks who know better. The list of Christian creeds is impressively long and complicated.

Take the case of the Christmas story. The story most of us know today is an amalgamation of different versions pulled from two of the gospels. In one, following the birth of Jesus, Mary and Joseph flee with their son from Bethlehem to Egypt when King Herod orders all the newborn infants to be killed because he fears a prophesy that one of these infants will grow up to supplant him as king of the Jews. In this gospel, they stay in Egypt for a number of years before traveling home to Nazareth.

In the other gospel Jesus, Mary and Joseph do not go to Egypt, but immediately travel straight home to Nazareth.

Both of these descriptions of the events following the birth of Jesus cannot be true, and there are literally hundreds of such contradictions.

God loves homosexuals; God hates homosexuals. God says don't kill; God says kill your own children if they leave the faith. God says it is easier for a camel to pass through the eye of a needle than for a rich man to enter the kingdom of heaven, and God says God wants you to be rich. God loves innocent children; God kills innocent children. God forgives all; God punishes you for the sins of your grandfathers even if you repent those sins you never committed. God says to love your neighbor; God says to kill your neighbor if he's a non-believer. God is the God of the Jews; God hates the Jews. You should only have one wife; you can have all the wives you want. Keep slaves; don't keep slaves. Don't commit genocide; kill all the Canaanites down to every last man, woman and child. Rape is bad; go ahead and rape the women of your enemies. All of this is in the Bible.

Anything you want to believe, you can find a justification for in the Bible. This is why we have so many different forms of faith that we loosely term "Christianity." You can believe anything at all and be a "Christian," so long as the word "Jesus" appears somewhere in your theology.

The Bible is a mirror. People see in the Bible reflections of themselves. If you think that the Bible is about God's love, then you will see that because there is plenty in the Bible that speaks of God's love.

If you think that the Bible is about strict rules set down by God that must be followed because God is wrathful but just, then that is what you find.

If you think that the Bible gives you free will to choose between good and evil, there is justification for that.

If you believe that the Bible says there is no free will and your God has preordained your fate, that is in the Bible, too.

If you want to be rich, God wants you to prosper. It says so in the Bible. If you think wealth and possessions are evil and the temptation of Satan, that's in the Bible, too.

Hold up the mirror and the reflection is a commentary on who you are.

From the legend of Narcissus: Narcissus in Greek mythology was a hunter who was renowned for his beauty. He was exceptionally proud, and he disdained those who loved him. Nemesis saw this and attracted Narcissus to a pool so he could see his own reflection in the water. He fell in love with it, not realizing it was merely an image, and unable to leave the beauty of his reflection, Narcissus died.

Institutional religions of all kinds—Christian, Jew, Muslim, Hindu, Buddhist and so forth—all rely on ancient books full of inconsistencies and contradictions that confuse and bedevil the poor human beings who try to use them to make sense out of their yearning for a spiritual life. And for people who are not careful, they look into the pool of religious dogma and fall in love with their own reflections instead of with God, and they worship themselves, not the creator of all things.

And so Muslims will blow themselves up in the name of God to kill infidels and even other "heretic" Muslims, and Christians will gleefully slaughter each other in Northern Ireland in the name of God, and Hindus and Muslims will massacre each other because God wills it, and so on through the bloody annals of history.

All of the blood and hate and stupidity must make God weep.

And so in the Church of the Holy Sepulcher I felt myself in the presence of Jesus, standing, if not in some of the places where he had actually been, at least close to them in a place that symbolically reminded me of what his life had been about, and I thought of what he stood for and what he died for and I admired him for it. His life is an inspiration of sacrifice, selflessness and forgiveness, which far too many Christians today prefer not to remember, and is a lesson very few people of faith, in my experience, have ever taken to heart.

CHAPTER 6

About this time a relative had a child, and Wes was going to return to the U.S. in time for the christening. I decided to send a special gift along.

I packed an empty bottle to take on the trip back to Jordan with the idea of collecting some Jordan River water for the baptism. It was not that I thought being baptized with that water made a child special in any way, or would grant him or her superpowers; it was simply that I liked the symbolism. It would add to the ritual, and ritual is an important part of what binds us together.

I was a little unsure, however, how to collect the water without being shot by the itchy-fingered troops on either side of the border. Wes and I discussed it and thought it might be best to try and get permission to go to the edge of the river and dip our bottle in the water.

We asked an Israeli guard about this, and he emphatically said, "No, no! Bombahs!" He made an exploding motion with his hands.

His English was poor, but we quickly realized he meant that the riverbank was heavily mined on both sides. It would be certain death to approach the River of Peace on foot. It seems not many people are baptized in the Jordan River these days.

So we drove to the middle of the bridge, where I once again changed license plates. Only this time, I pulled out my empty bottle and a length of rope. I tied the rope securely around the neck of the bottle and tossed it into the river from the middle of the bridge.

I felt itchy doing it, and could see the soldiers on both sides starring at us, wondering just what the hell we were doing. Wes tried waving to them while smiling broadly, indicating that we were just a couple of crazy Americans and to pay no attention to us, or if they had to watch, at least not to shoot us.

The bottle sank in the green water, and I pulled it back up, capped it, threw it in the trunk, and we were on our way back home, none the worse for wear and not aerated with bullet holes.

Wes brought the water back and I later heard that the minister did not want to use it. There were several babies being baptized, and he thought it would make the other parents feel bad if my nephew was baptized with Jordan River water while their kids were not. Besides, he said, it had a kind of voodoo feel to it, because it did not matter what water you used for baptism. Just like me, he knew it was not going to bestow superpowers on the child. He might also have said that, given how polluted the water was, it probably was not even healthy.

My sister in law was having none of it, however. She said her brother in law had risked his damn neck getting that water for this baptism, and they were going to by god use it.

Besides, she said, he could use the water to baptize all the babies that day, so no one had to feel slighted or upstaged.

The minister gave in.

My nephew, I can report today, does not have superpowers, but the water did not poison him, either.

I still think that there is an alien watching all this from space who is about ready to give up trying to figure out what the hell this planet is all about.

CHAPTER 7

Khartoum, the capital of Sudan, sits at the confluence of the White and Blue Niles. The White Nile flows out of the south, from deep in the heart of Africa, and was the object of years of investigation by some of history's most famous and eccentric explorers, seeking its source.

The Blue Nile originates in the highlands of Ethiopia. It spills swiftly down out of the mountains to Khartoum, where it unites with the White Nile. From there, the combined rivers flow to the north into Egypt and finally the Mediterranean Sea.

It sounds romantic. It was not. When I arrived in Khartoum in 1992, it was one of the most derelict, rundown and decrepit capital cities in the world. The area around Khartoum is mostly desert, and periodically sandstorms of biblical proportion blow in.

The roads were in awful shape, and when it rained you avoided driving into any pool of water. You never knew how deep it was, and whole cars sometimes were swallowed up. As far as electricity went, the city power grid was off more often than it was on.

Osama bin Laden was living near Khartoum at that time, as was the terrorist Carlos the Jackal. An American ambassador had, several years before, been assassinated in Khartoum by Palestinian terrorists.

The leader of the Sudan in 1992 was Hassan al-Turabi, the Islamic extremist of the National Islamic Front, or NIF.

As awful and miserable a place as the Sudan was in 1992, that did not stop the Sudanese, especially those in the government, from harboring the most amazing delusions about the position Sudan held in the world.

I was invited one day to attend the opening ceremonies for a new museum in Omdurman, the twin city of Khartoum. Around 1881, an Islamic leader called the Mahdi (the expected one) led a revolt against British control. This revolt stunned Britain by successfully defeating its forces in a battle that made the British General, previously known as Charles "Chinese" Gordon, forever famous as Gordon of Khartoum. He, and all his mostly local troops, were massacred in Khartoum by the Mahdi's forces. It would be almost twenty years before the British returned, with a young Winston Churchill as a member of the army, to defeat the new rulers of the Sudan and reassert British dominance. For you movie buffs, in the epic Hollywood version of this story called *Khartoum*, Charlton Heston plays a very taciturn Gordon and Laurence Olivier plays a sinister Mahdi. While the plot is predictably seriously biased against the Mahdi, the movie is fun and not completely inaccurate.

The centerpiece of the new museum was a complex of buildings that had housed the Mahdi and his successor's government (the Mahdi died not long after the fall of Khartoum to his forces) until the return of the British. I was surprised to be invited to the opening, given the naturally anti-foreign tenor of the event. When I arrived, however, I was given a place of honor in the front row and handed a cold Coke. A large tent erected in front of the new museum contained an enthusiastic crowd from all walks of life in Khartoum.

The speechifying began in Arabic with a series of dignitaries making astonishing assertions. As I looked around at the hot, dusty and blighted landscape, I was told that Sudan was acknowledged by all nations to be the center of the world. I was told that everyone was at this very moment looking to Khartoum as the leader of a new world order, a moral order that had been born in the Sudan with the Mahdi, a hero whose vision was today coming to fruition thanks to the leadership of Sudan. Even the Queen of England would be forced to bow down in London facing toward Khartoum, which was already acknowledged to be the center of the new Islamic rebirth. In fact, the shining success of Islam in Sudan, as handed down by the Mahdi, would inspire people everywhere to flock to the Muslim faith.

The decadent Western world was on its knees. Its armies would no longer fight. Its corrupt and exploitative economic system could no longer sustain the West's bloated and wasteful lifestyle. Soon, Sudan would triumph over its enemies in the West and all Muslims everywhere would come in a great stampede to Khartoum, the shining city on the hill of the new world order.

I sat drinking my Coke and kept looking up and down the dust-choked street of this shabby, broken-down town. A wildly cheering audience periodically interrupted the speakers by jumping to their feet, praising God and shaking swords in the air. I had not noticed the swords before, and now everyone seemed to have one.

When the speeches ended, the crowd rushed to the gates of the museum to revel in the glories of the past. Before they were permitted in, however, they had to allow the dignitaries to lead the way. To my surprise, the organizers rushed over, grabbed me, and insisted that I, as an honored guest, should be among the first to enter. They forced the crowd apart and pushed me through.

I did not like it. The crowd, agitated by the anti-foreign rhetoric and the pride they felt in their past martial accomplishments, clearly did not understand why I, a foreign infidel, was led to the front of the line. Faces scowled with undisguised hostility at me, and many of those faces belonged to people whose hands were gripping big, sharp swords.

I had no desire to be the star in a ritual re-enactment of the slaughter of General Gordon at the hands of the Mahdi's zealots, as poetic as that might have been as the final act to the opening ceremonies for the Mahdi's museum.

However, with loud haranguing by the organizers, I made it through the crowd and safely into the museum. Once everyone was in, the crowd forgot about me and I was left to roam the complex at my leisure.

The museum was actually well done. The buildings had been, on the whole, nicely restored, and the exhibits were informative and interesting, if predictably biased. Hell, if Hollywood could stretch the truth a little about General Gordon, I could hardly begrudge the same privilege to the Sudanese and the Mahdi.

I was to return to Sudan on assignment some fifteen years later. By 2008, Khartoum had completely transformed into a modern and bustling city. Oil had been discovered in the southern half of the country. South Sudan received little benefit from it, but oil wealth stolen from the southerners allowed the government in Khartoum to transform the capital into a prosperous, modern city.

CHAPTER 8

After Khartoum, I was assigned to our new embassy in the new nation of Eritrea, in east Africa. There are many things about Eritrea that made it different from anywhere else I have lived.

One clue about this is that although it is on the Red Sea with a long coastline and bountiful marine life, it was a place where people had forgotten how to fish. It was also a place where we had a U.S. embassy library, even though the U.S. government had not run a cultural affairs office there in over twenty years.

In the great colonial land grabs in Africa, Eritrea wound up as an Italian possession until after World War II, when the victorious British army took it over. When the British let it go, it was annexed to Ethiopia by the United Nations, very much against the will of the Eritrean people. The U.N. mandated that Eritrea should maintain a semi-autonomous status inside the Ethiopian federal system, as a sop to the Eritreans, but no one was surprised when Haile Selassie, the Emperor of Ethiopia, abolished the Eritrean legislature and ended its special status in the empire.

The Eritreans simply refused to be annexed, and they fought a thirty-year war for independence, beginning around 1960.

In the comic-opera political maneuvering of the Cold War, we started out supporting Haile Selassie and the Ethiopians. This was partly because the Emperor allowed the U.S. Army to build a large U.S. listening post in Eritrea, enabling us to eavesdrop on all Soviet military activity moving through or near the Red Sea, a strategic choke point for the shipment of oil from the Persian Gulf through the Suez Canal.

Haile Selassie is an all-too-typical example of a leader who starts out with the potential for greatness, and often does great things early on, but then forever hangs on to power until he becomes so corrupt, out of touch, and often simply crazy that even Mother Theresa would shoot him dead.

Emperor Selassie was forced aside (and reportedly later suffocated to make it appear he had died in his sleep) by a particularly nasty piece of work named Mengistu Haile Mariam.

Although several groups were involved in the overthrow, Mengistu assumed power as head of state after murdering his competitors, and he was just getting warmed up. Mengistu did not bother to start out good; he jumped straight into the homicidal lunatic category of leadership.

Mengistu decided early on to be a Communist, and so naturally Ethiopia ceased to be an ally of the U.S. and became an ally of the Soviet Union.

In reality, Mengistu was not a Communist, he was just a brutal, paranoid, psychopathic freak who nationalized all foreign-owned and most domestic companies without compensation so that he could own it all himself. It used to be called being an absolute monarch, but he wanted Soviet support so he called it Communism.

Mengistu is probably most famous for the period in Ethiopia known as the "red terror," during which thousands of his suspected enemies (and it did not take much to be suspected) were tortured and killed. When students rioted in protest, many were shot and their parents sent bills ordering them to pay for the bullets that killed their children.

The Eritreans did very well militarily against the Ethiopian army, which, as you can imagine, was not a highly motivated fighting force. The rebels were on the verge of winning their independence when Mengistu became a "Communist." The Soviets then propped him up with massive amounts of military assistance, resulting in the war dragging on for another fifteen years, with all the death, misery and destruction that so needlessly went along with it.

Meanwhile, on the other side of Ethiopia, Somalia, which had been a Soviet ally, switched sides in the Cold War and became our good friend. We took over the old Soviet naval base in Somalia, allowing us to keep our military window on the region until Somalia fell apart and essentially ceased to be a nation state, although by then the Cold War was over so it did not particularly matter to Russian or American spies. Ironically, the only ones who seemed to feel bad about all this were the Cubans, who had been helping the Eritreans when Ethiopia was an ally of the U.S., and who were then asked by the Soviets to help the Ethiopians when they switched sides. The Cubans seemed to think this was wrong.

In May of 1991, the Mengistu government finally collapsed. Mengistu later bitterly blamed this on Mikhail Gorbachev because he was responsible, according to Mengistu, for letting the Soviet Union collapse, which ended Soviet funding for the Mengistu government, without which he could not survive.

Unfortunately, Mengistu was not imprisoned when his government fell, as he so richly deserved. He fled and was granted asylum in Zimbabwe by that other great African lunatic and leader for life, the only recently deposed President Robert Mugabe. At the time of this writing, Mengistu still resides there despite attempts by Ethiopia to extradite him to face trial for war crimes. President Mugabe said the accusations were a fabrication of the Western powers. According to him, everything bad always was.

But that does not explain how the Eritreans forgot how to fish. The reason was that the Ethiopians banned fishing during the long war to stop Eritrean rebels from smuggling arms into the country on fishing boats. The Eritreans did it anyway, but the ban made it harder. The only real result was that the Eritreans forgot how to fish, and had to learn again after the war.

And then there is the question of why the Eritreans had an American government library in Asmara, the capital of Eritrea, even after Mengistu ordered the American Consulate in Asmara closed in 1976.

The American Consulate in Asmara had a U.S. library and when the American director left, he handed the keys to Kefela Kokobu, a local employee, and told him to take care of the books. He did for seventeen years until I arrived in 1994 after Eritrean independence, when we opened a U.S. embassy in Asmara.

Now here is a lesson in what American public diplomacy is all about. When I arrived in Asmara, one of the first things I did was to visit what was still called the American Library, even though there had been no American there for seventeen years and we had not contributed a penny to its support in all that time. Kefela took me on a tour of the facility.

The library was a time capsule of what a U.S. embassy library had been seventeen years earlier. Even though it was a circulating library, all of the books were still there. They were dog-eared, worn and very, very used from being read by thousands of Eritreans, but almost none had been lost or stolen.

In order not to be executed by Mengistu's government, Kefela had invited the Soviets to donate any books that they wanted and he added them to the collection.

They gave him many books, and Kefela showed them to me. They were in pristine condition. That was because, Kefela explained, they had not been touched or opened. Nobody wanted to read them.

What they wanted to read was *Huckleberry Finn* and the Norton Anthology of American Short Stories. They wanted to read about American history and American social sciences and American political thinking and American business practices and American education. They drank it up.

When Mengistu's henchmen came through and ordered Kefela to take books off the self that they deemed corrupting, Kefela took them off the shelves until they left, and then he put them back.

He could have been shot for it, but he kept that library going, that *American* library, year after lonely year, without pay or support from the American government. For seventeen years he "took care of those books."

When I arrived in 1994, there was no reason why the Eritreans should have welcomed me. The Americans had supported the Ethiopians until Mengistu took over. Even after that, we never lifted a finger to help the Eritreans, although they were the enemy of our enemy. No one much helped the Eritreans at all, and perhaps that was a blessing in the end, because if the Eritreans had become anything after all that time, they were self-reliant, even to a fault.

But I am convinced one of the reasons we were well thought of and remembered was because of Kefela and the American Library he kept open all of those years. It was my great honor to get to know and work with him. He was the first person I hired on to my new staff.

I thought he had earned it.

CHAPTER 9

Kefela once told me a joke about himself. Asmara was frequently shelled during the war, although it was seldom clear which side was doing it. On one occasion, artillery rounds fell randomly across the city, sending inhabitants scrambling in every direction.

Kefela just stood on a street corner calmly peering up at the sky. A friend running by stopped in amazement and asked him what he was doing.

"I'm looking for the rocket that's going to land on my head," he replied.

"Are you crazy?" shouted his friend, and he ran off.

This is an Eritrean style joke. The point of it is that there was no safety in running around like a headless chicken when shells were falling randomly. If one had your name written on it, your time was up, so you might as well stand to watch it coming for you.

I confess I don't have that kind of equilibrium in the face of extinction.

When I arrived in Eritrea, it was impossible to miss the sad and often nightmarish signs of war. Destroyed Ethiopian tanks, trucks and ammunition, both used and live, littered the countryside. There were so many land mines still in the ground you could only safely walk in the rural areas on cow and sheep paths. Step off and you risked losing a leg or worse.

I stopped on a bridge once and saw in the dry ravine it crossed the skeleton of a camel and, not far from it, a man. The areas around bridges were often heavily mined to keep the Eritrean rebels from ambushing military convoys crossing them. The flesh of the man had disintegrated long ago, but his ragged uniform still clung to his sun-bleached bones. It was obvious from his position that he had not died outright, but had attempted to crawl out of his trap. No one could get to him, however, to help. Even as I stood there, it would have been suicide to walk out to his body.

Just outside the port city of Masawa on the Red Sea was a place they called the bone tree, a lone tree not far from the road in the middle of a hot dry plain. The remains of about fifty Ethiopian army officers surrounded it. During the war, there had been a revolt in the military against Mengistu. It failed and Mengistu ordered all the officers in the affected units shot. The executions were carried out under this tree.

I went to look. It was the kind of horror I could not help but witness. Still in their uniforms, skeleton was heaped upon skeleton exactly where they had fallen and been left as a warning to others. Wedding rings still hung on finger bones and disconnected leg femurs thrust up from boots now empty except for the loose remains of anklebones. Skulls stared with empty eye sockets at the clear blue sky.

One reason the Ethiopian army performed so poorly in the war was that officers who failed in assignments were routinely executed. Everyone fails sometime, so the officer corps was decimated, demoralized and terrified. The common soldier was usually a conscript who, not uncommonly, had been playing soccer with his friends at school when an army truck pulled up, armed men jumped out and all the boys were forced into the trucks, never to see their families again. They were given about a month of training and then sent to the front.

On several occasions I walked along an old Ethiopian battle line. I had to stick right to the trench line itself, because not only did the Ethiopians mine the area in front of them against attackers, but they mined the area behind them, too, to discourage retreat. Most of these places were also littered with the bones of the dead. Littered seems a poor word to use when describing the bodies of men killed in combat. After all, they were not candy wrappers or discarded soda cans. But, sadly, that is what it was like for the remains of those Ethiopian soldiers.

And so, although the Eritreans were far fewer in number, with far less equipment and little outside support, they won this long, hard war. They were all volunteers fighting to make a country, while the Ethiopians were fighting for a government that treated them like the cannon fodder it so obviously thought them to be. One Eritrean ex-fighter (they did not call themselves soldiers because they were unpaid volunteers, and were, therefore, "fighters") and his ex-fighter wife became good friends of mine: Danny and Abrehat.

Danny was short and compact, while Abrehat was taller and slim. Few Eritreans are heavy. Both of them had joined the liberation army very young. Danny was about fifteen, although he told the army he was older, and his first rifle was as tall as he was.

Abrehat was about thirteen. The rebel army refused to take her. The Eritreans did not knowingly use child soldiers. They sent her home, and she came back. They sent her home again, and she came back again. They gave up and put her in a school they operated for the children of fighters. When she was old enough, they finally admitted her into the army.

It's big news that American women are allowed to take combat assignments in the U.S. armed forces. There are those who say women are not suited to combat. They don't know Eritrea. About 30% of the Eritrean army was staffed by women. The Eritreans were so outnumbered by the larger Ethiopia that the leadership felt they had no choice but to admit women into the army. The women served alongside the men in every capacity, including combat. In the army, they were complete equals. This is even more remarkable considering that Eritrea was a traditional African/Arab culture about evenly split between Christians and Muslims. Up to the time of the war, women were expected to stay at home and be housewives.

In the case of Abrehat, one of the reasons she kept running away from home was that she wanted to be a singer. Her father was a singer, but when he caught her singing at home, he beat her. It was not proper for a woman to aspire to be a singer. He thought it would disgrace the family.

In the army, Abrehat became a famous singer. The Eritreans had a clandestine radio station, and her patriotic songs in support of the war were popular across the country. Like most fighters, however, she did not use her real name during the war to prevent reprisals against family members by the Ethiopian authorities.

The irony of this was that her father became a huge fan of hers, and he did not learn until after the war that it was his own daughter he so admired.

But Abrehat was also a fighter. Her singing was something she did when she could be spared from the front. From all accounts, the women of Eritrea were excellent soldiers and deadly in combat.

I once was asked to speak to a group of ex-fighters who were in a class to improve their English. I spoke about the United States, and then took their questions.

They had several questions concerning why the United States had not helped them during the war, since they were fighting a Communist government in Ethiopia.

I told them that it had not been our fight, and that it was better for outsiders not to meddle in regional conflicts of this sort. In the end, they had won and they could say that they had done it on their own. That kind of self-reliance would serve them well. They were an independent country, beholden to no one, and, although it had been a long and difficult struggle, to be self-reliant was a price worth paying.

It was kind of true.

When I finished with that, I had the chance to question them. About a third of the class was composed of women.

I asked them how the Ethiopians reacted to facing women in combat during the war. The women smirked and the men furrowed their brows. Finally, one of the men answered, "It scared them."

Everyone nodded.

I thought that an odd response. Why, I asked, did the women scare them?

"Because," answered another man, "they had deeper beliefs. They felt the war harder."

I said I did not know what that meant.

There was silence for a few moments, and then a man answered, "They had less mercy for the Ethiopians than the Eritrean men. The women knew what would happen to them if they were captured, and it made them fight harder. They were fierce in combat."

Then one fellow raised his hand and said, "I would like to tell a story of what happened to me."

I urged him to go ahead.

He stood and made a formal presentation, rather like someone reciting a verse by his favorite poet.

During the war, he said, he had been assigned to help smuggle ammunition and equipment into Eritrea by sea. He made many successful runs, but on the last trip, an Ethiopian patrol boat overtook them. Eritreans were not supposed to be out on the water, and the boat was full of arms. He knew they were doomed.

When the patrol boat got close enough, he and his comrades opened fire, but it was armored and they did little damage. Armed with much bigger guns, the patrol boat backed off and began raking them with heavy machinegun fire. His boat was rapidly torn to pieces and his comrades slaughtered. There were three women fighters with them. The women, he said, decided the Ethiopians would not take them alive. They tied themselves together, grabbed some heavy objects that they fixed to themselves and then jumped over the side of the boat.

The attack continued until their boat disintegrated. Miraculously, he was not hit, and he hid under the wreckage. The patrol boat did not come close, the sailors not wanting to risk taking fire, and when they satisfied themselves there were no survivors, they left.

He emerged and, to his surprise, found one other survivor. He built a crude raft from the remains of the boat, constructed a crude sail and urged his comrade to join him. Driven insane by the shock of the attack, the man refused, and nothing he said or did would coax this fellow onto his raft; there was nothing to do but leave.

He never saw him again.

He drifted on the open sea for about a day and a half before being rescued. The most frightening time was at night, he said, when his raft was knocked about by some creature in the water, he did not know what.

When he got back, he refused to go to sea again and was transferred to another job.

He sat down, and the class was quiet for a while. The fellow just stared at his hands.

After the class, I learned that this had been the first time he had ever told the story of what had happened to him that day, other than to say that he was the only survivor.

I heard many, many stories like this from both men and women, stories of personal survival in impossible situations in which most, if not all, of their comrades were lost. The Eritreans paid a heavy price for their independence.

CHAPTER 10

One factor that made Eritrea a great assignment was Ambassador Robert Houdek. Bob knew the region, had an excellent relationship with the government of Eritrea, understood the Eritrean character and was a supportive supervisor. Ambassadors are like seventeenth-century ship captains, with not quite the power of life and death over the staff of an embassy, but close to it.

Bob had been ambassador in Uganda when rebels attacked the capital and overthrew the government. He was the chief of mission at our embassy in Ethiopia when Mengistu was finally thrown out. So he had seen his fair share of killing and war. Opening our embassy in Eritrea was his last job before retirement. He could have had a higher prestige post, but Eritrea was where he wanted to be. He knew how hard these people had fought to make a country, and he wanted to see what they would do now that they had it.

The problem with the Eritrean government, Bob once told me, was that it was composed, naturally, of the men and women who had led the long rebel fight against Ethiopia, and at the top of them all was Isaias Afwerki, the former rebel supreme commander made president. A George Washington of his country.

The problem was twofold. George Washington had the wisdom to step down after eight years, and the skills needed to lead a successful fight for independence are often not the same ones needed to lead a nation, but in our case Washington also had political leadership skills. It's about twenty-five years since Isaias took over, and he is a poor leader; for tens of thousands of Eritreans, his flaws would be fatal.

I met President Isaias three days after arriving in the country. The ambassador had an appointment with him to discuss signing an agreement to establish a Peace Corps program, and he invited me along to be his note-taker for the meeting, although the real reason was to give me a chance to meet the president.

Isaias in 1994 was tall and youthful in appearance, without a sign of gray in his dark black hair and moustache, although he was close to fifty years old at the time. He was already considered a maverick among African leaders for his tendency to bluntly speak his mind, especially about the failings of other African heads of state. Eritrea, he promised, was going to be different. There would be no corruption, no cult of the leader and the government would set priorities and stick to them.

At first, that was the way it worked. It was refreshing. Corruption, the plague of African governance, was almost unknown. In most African countries, the head of state considers the job his for life. Elections are window dressing mounted largely to placate western donor demands for giving the appearance of a commitment to democratic principles. Images of the Great Leader appear on everything from the money to billboards to every empty wall where a poster can be pasted.

Isaias did none of those things. I seldom saw his photo at all. Eritrea carefully thought out a national development plan, and then stuck to it. A poor country, the leadership knew it had limited managerial capacity to direct new projects, making it essential to keep focused on national priorities and not get distracted. It is the only African country I know that turned down aid money. If the project was not a priority, they felt, rightly, it was better not to lose a good manager to do something of lesser importance to national development.

A classic example was food aid. The new government did not want foreign governments passing out free food. In many places in Africa, that is how food aid is managed, and it creates an "aid dependency" mentality. Eritrea insisted that food be turned over to the government to sell on the open market. The government then used the money to pay people to do public works projects to improve the infrastructure of the country, which had largely been demolished by the war. That way, instead of getting a handout, the people worked for the improvement of their nation and were paid for it, breeding pride instead of dependence.

I agreed with the approach, and so did, I am glad to say, the U.S. government, which cooperated with the program. The Europeans, however, refused. And so the Eritreans turned down their aid. If it was not to be given on their terms, they did not want it. They would find some other way to get the people fed that did not turn them into parasites instead of productive workers.

The beginning of the failure of Eritrean leadership to make the change from a revolutionary movement in the field to a national government occurred when, in December of 1995, Eritrea came to blows with Yemen over the Hanish Islands at the southern opening to the Red Sea. There is not much to the Hanish Islands. They are barren rocks with little except for the occasional fishing boat that stops there, and on the largest of the islands a small resort facility for tourists interested in scuba diving.

In short, not the kind of place one normally thinks most people would be willing to risk getting killed over. But of course people did.

The Eritreans contended that the islands belonged to them, and the Yemenis held the opposite view. One day, nearly out of the blue, the Yemenis decided to assert their claim by placing 300 troops on the largest of the islands.

The islands are so isolated that the Eritreans did not even notice the presence of the Yemenis for several days. When they finally did, they landed their own smaller contingent of troops at the other end of the island. It took the Yemenis a few days to figure out that the Eritreans were there. Up to this point, this was a comedy.

It did not stay a comedy. Once the Yemenis discovered the Eritreans, fighting started. No one can say with certainty what actually happened. The Yemenis have their story, and the Eritreans tell a different one. From what I know of both sides, this is what I think happened. The Yemenis attacked the Eritreans to force them off the island. The Eritreans were dug in and did not respond other than to defend their position. I have toured Eritrean battlefields and can attest to the fact that they are very good, indeed, at taking up a defensive position. However, a lucky mortar round landed in the Eritrean camp, killed a couple of soldiers, and that angered the Eritreans sufficiently that they counterattacked. When it was over, the Yemenis were routed, all of them either killed or captured, and of that fact there is no dispute.

Naturally, the Yemenis were humiliated. It would have been far better had the two sides simply ignored each other, or, having come to blows, that the fight had resulted in a stand-off. But now Yemeni national honor was wounded. The possible repercussions for the Yemeni government were staggering, even for the Eritreans, but the Eritrean leadership saw the issue in simple terms. They thought they owned the islands. The Yemenis had tried to seize them by force, and they responded to secure their rights. The Eritreans said that if anyone could prove they did not own the islands, they would withdraw, and they were willing to submit their claim to binding international arbitration.

It sounds reasonable. It was not. What it ignored were the political repercussions of what they had done and the consequences of the Yemeni defeat for the Yemeni government. While that government was not a democracy, on the whole it was fairly enlightened at that time. Eritrea lives in a troubled neighborhood with many unstable and often outright hostile neighbors, including Sudan, Ethiopia and Djibouti, with Saudi Arabia and Yemen facing them across the Red Sea. Eritrea had just emerged from a long war and could not afford to become embroiled in another over territory that was not worth the spilling a single drop of blood.

Further, Eritrea refused to take into account that the government in Yemen was seriously threatened by extremist Muslim elements using the humiliation of Yemeni forces to attack those in power.

Eritrea, being approximately half Muslim and half Christian, did fear (and for good reason) the emergence of Muslim extremists seeking to polarize the country and create civil strife. They already suspected the Sudanese of supporting just such an extremist group that was making occasional cross border raids into Eritrea at that time.

What Eritrea was doing in the Hanish Islands threatened to create a hostile Islamic state across the Red Sea that would spend years stoking internal conflict in Eritrea.

During this time, Ambassador Houdek left the country to attend an important regional conference. He put me in charge of the embassy in his absence, with tongue-in-cheek strict instructions not to let the situation spin out of control. In fact, it did get worse and I was forced at one point to speak to the Foreign Minister, emphasizing that being right was not as important as considering what was best for the country, and stressing the importance of providing a face-saving diplomatic solution for the Yemeni government.

The Foreign Minister was Petros Solomon. He had been a long-time leader in the independence struggle, and was a good, reasonable man. I liked him. He listened to what I had to say, agreed that the internal situation in Yemen was dire and said he would do what he could. It turned out not to be much. Isaias considered the internal strife of the Yemenis to be their problem, and he would not back down.

This time, they were lucky. In the end, the Yemeni government survived the crisis, and accepted to go to binding arbitration. In 1998, the international arbitration panel awarded the Hanish Islands to Yemen, and Eritrea withdrew its forces exactly as promised.

As far as Isaias was concerned, Eritrea took the honorable course and kept to its word. He had nothing to apologize for.

It is true that Eritrea kept to its word, but its actions had not been wise. It was gaining a reputation in the neighborhood for shooting first and asking questions later while making enemies it could not afford.

In the next confrontation, it was not so lucky.

Most people would assume that after thirty years of war, it was natural that Ethiopia and Eritrea would be mortal enemies who could be expected to come to blows again. The surprise was the situation was the opposite.

The new Prime Minister of Ethiopia at that time, Meles Zenawi, and President Isaisas of Eritrea went to college together and were friends. Meles went on to lead the rebel movement inside Ethiopia that eventually succeeded in overthrowing the Mengistu regime, while Isaisas led the Eritrean independence movement. While they were "in the field," they stayed in contact and supported each other whenever they could. It is said that there were Eritrean rebel units in the offensive that finally took Addis Ababa, Ethiopia's capital.

After the overthrow of Mengistu, Meles took a great deal of heat internally for not vigorously opposing Eritrean independence. Worst of all for the Ethiopians, the new Eritrean nation took Ethiopia's entire former coastline, leaving it a landlocked country.

When I was in Eritrea, most people I knew spoke of the closeness of the two governments, and that eventually they would probably form some kind of economic union. The Ethiopians had special rights to transship goods coming into the now Eritrean seaport of Asab, which became the main seaport for Ethiopia.

As examples of productive regional cooperation and commitment to a new style of governance in Africa, both Isaisas and Meles were held up as a new generation of leaders on the continent who held the promise of a new start for these desperately poor nations.

That cooperation was destroyed by a border dispute and another serious miscalculation on the part of the Eritrean government on how to handle it. This time, it cost them.

When Eritrea became independent, much of its border was not clearly defined, at least as far as its neighbors were concerned. Eritrea has always had a very clear idea of where it considers its borders to be.

On the border between Eritrea and Ethiopia is a small, no-account town called Badme, a place in the middle nowhere on the edge of nothing. For a half-million dollars, you could buy all the disputed land and still have change left over, but no one in his right mind would ever want to purchase the place. It's not desert, but it is dry and dusty most of the year, with little to recommend it.

Eritrea claimed it. Ethiopia administered it. One unfortunate day Eritrean policemen entered the town to assert their administrative claim, a fight broke out, and a couple of them were killed.

What Isaisas should have done was to call his good buddy Meles and ask him just what the hell he was doing on their border. He did not.

What he did do was to send a large unit of Eritrean army personnel, with tanks and heavy equipment, into the town to seize it.

Once again, in the mind of Isaisis, this land belonged to Eritrea and he would suffer no question about it. He was again willing to submit the claim to international arbitration, and if proven wrong, he would surrender the town back to Ethiopia.

Again, this catastrophically ignored what Isaisis had just done to his friend Meles. From Meles's point of view, Isaisis had stabbed him in the back and was trying to kill him, and that could well have been the result because Isaisis again refused to consider the internal political situation faced by Meles.

Both Ethiopia and Eritrea include several major ethnic groups. Meles belonged to the Tigrean tribe. His army during the rebellion against the Ethiopian government was called the Tigrean People's

Liberation Front (TPLF). The Tigres represented barely a tenth of the population, but when the TPLF came to power it refused to share it in any meaningful way with most of the other ethnic groups. This was typical for Ethiopia, which previously had been dominated by the ethnic group known as the Amharas.

Naturally, Meles's government was unpopular with the old Amhara elites, and he had to face armed opposition from other ethnically based movements excluded from power. These divisions were made worse by the development of an intense rivalry within the TPLF between moderates and the most nationalistic Tigreans, which Meles was powerless to avoid. To the extent he could, he kept these extremist Tigreans out of the national government in Addis Ababa and left them to run the Tigre Regional State.

The Tigre Regional State borders Eritrea, and many ethnic Tigreans live on the Eritrean side of the border. These nationalistic Tigreans wanted to appropriate as much of the Tigre sections of Eritrea as they could, since they believed all Tigreans should be a part of the Tigre Regional State in Ethiopia. It is also true that they were making trouble on the border with Eritrea, and the Eritreans were getting tired of it. These Tigreans may even have been behind the murder of the Eritrean police that sparked the conflict.

But by preemptively seizing the territory instead of working with Meles, Isaisas put him in an impossible situation politically. Meles, already the head of a minority government, could under no circumstances alienate his Tigrean base. If he did not stand up to the Eritreans militarily, at best his government would have been overthrown, and at worst the extremists in his own party would have assassinated him. The last was by far the most likely outcome.

Meles knew that Isaisas was aware of all of this. So far as Meles was concerned, therefore, Isaisas was trying to kill him. Not only did Meles have no political choice but to declare war on Eritrea once again, but now it was a grudge match between two former friends turned mortal enemies.

Both countries spent tens of millions of dollars that neither could afford on arms and munitions. By my estimation, at least 100,000 died in the war.

When enough territory had been gained by the Ethiopians to save face, and when enough blood had been spilled on both sides, and when most of the money they possessed had been wasted on arms, then both sides finally agreed to a U.N.-brokered cease-fire and to binding U.N.-sponsored arbitration on the delineation of the border.

It turned out, Badme did belong to Eritrea. Not that it mattered. A hundred Badmes would not have been worth the misery, death, waste and destruction.

Prominent members of his government, already disillusioned by the military catastrophe, told Isaisas he was on the wrong track for the country. These people had spent years, and sometimes decades, in the field with Isaisas fighting for their country. Petros Solomon, the Foreign Minister I mentioned earlier, was among them.

Isaias put them all in jail, many of them for doing no more than suggesting that he should not have closed the independent press, which he had recently done to silence their criticism of him. Not only did he jail them, but just like Mengistu before him, many of the detainees simply disappeared. It has now been years since anyone has seen Petros Solomon. There is an excellent chance he was murdered.

Well over half the people I know have fled the country, people who sacrificed everything for independence. Others would leave if they could, but it is difficult to get out. You need government permission to cross the border or get on a plane.

And so Isaias has simply become another African megalomaniac, increasingly out of touch with the country he should have served, but instead has come to brutalize. A man who could have been remembered as one of the founding fathers of a new Africa, his fixation on his own political survival has doomed him to become the exact thing he fought so long to bring down: a shabby, murderous tyrant.

CHAPTER 11

One day in August of 1994, I was walking down the street near my office talking to an Eritrean journalist I was sending to the U.S. on a study tour for three weeks. He was an ex-fighter who had served in the war for independence for over fifteen years. A big guy, rather taller than me, most people would probably have found his appearance intimidating. He had fought in countless battles, and once told me that he never expected to survive the war. At this particular moment he had a tight hold of my hand. Men often walked around Asmara holding hands. It was what good male friends did. Still, I felt a bit odd and amused to be holding hands with this fierce-looking guy.

I got to my office and resumed work. It was another glorious day in Asmara, sunny and not too hot.

Then the phone rang.

I picked it up to find Neil Walsh on the other end, the Deputy Director of my home office in Washington.

"How's your French?" he asked.

"Not that good," I answered. "It's been ten years since I've had a chance to use it." I paused. "Why do I have the feeling you're not thinking about sending me to Paris?"

That night when I got home, I sat down with my wife and a martini and said, "I'm going to Rwanda tomorrow."

She laughed. "Sure. And I'm going to the moon."

"No," I said, "really. Washington called. They need someone to go to help reopen the embassy."

The terrible genocide that hit Rwanda in 1994 had only just happened. Our embassy in Kigali had closed and been evacuated during the height of the cataclysm. Aid was now rushing into the country, along with U.S. troops, and our embassy was about to reopen. They needed good officers to go help out.

My wife's face paled. "You're not kidding," she said.

The life of a Foreign Service officer can start a day one way, and end it in quite another.

CHAPTER 12

My first stop on my way to Kigali was Nairobi, Kenya, where I met with U.S. military planners to discuss the situation in Rwanda. I then went on to Kampala, Uganda, where I met T.J., the embassy Public Affairs Officer, a large man with a moustache and eyes that crinkled at the corners when he laughed, which was often. T.J. told me he had received a cryptic phone call from Neil Walsh in Washington that "if the situation in Rwanda was still thought to be dangerous, I was not to proceed until Neil got a piece of paper." T.J. had no idea what piece of paper he was talking about.

I said Neil could get all the pieces of paper he wanted; I still was not going to go into any danger area.

The next morning found me in the military section of Entebbe Airport trying to catch a ride into Rwanda on a U.S. military flight. Entebbe had a new terminal, but the military section where our American troops were stationed was next door to the old one. This was the location of the Israeli raid that freed over a hundred Jewish and Israeli hostages from a hijacked Air France flight that was forced to land there in June of 1976. The incident was made famous in two movies (and recently a third). Charles Bronson starred in one of them.

The weird thing was that eighteen years later the old terminal was still all shot-up, and the hijacked plane was still sitting next to it. It was so badly damaged Air France never tried to get it back.

I sat at the military airport and waited for the next flight for Kigali, along with about five journalists and several doctors trying to get

GUARDIANS OF THE GRAIL

to Goma, a small town on the Zaire-Rwandan border where thousands of Rwandan refugees were dying of cholera and exposure. At one point I got on a transport plane and was strapped in, ready to go, when at the last minute they decided to send that plane directly to Goma and everyone going to Kigali disembarked.

By the end of the day I was told that the next flight out would be at 6:00 A.M. the next morning, but I would need to be at the airport by 4:00 A.M., so I decided to just stay in the hanger and sleep on a military cot I was offered.

Surprisingly, Kampala is very cool, and I was downright cold during the night until a U.S. serviceman took pity on me and gave me a blanket from his pack.

The next morning, I did get out on a cargo flight along with about fifty U.S. Air Force guys headed to Kigali to secure the airport and get it fully functioning again. Their main task was to establish an air traffic control system and repair the runway lights to enable planes with relief supplies to land twenty-four hours a day. They accomplished this mission in twelve hours. These guys were good.

I arrived in Kigali at 8:00 in the morning, followed not long after by U.S. Secretary of Defense William Perry and a planeload of his hangers-on. Fortunately for me, the military Public Affairs Officers were responsible for handling the press swarming Perry, although it did give me the chance to meet the new leader of Rwanda, General Paul Kagame.

The genocide in Rwanda was rooted in conflicts between the two dominant ethnic groups in that country, the Hutus and the Tutsis. On taking power, Kagame, an ethnic Tutsi, took on the vice-presidency of Rwanda and the defense ministry, leaving the presidency to a man who was an ethnic Hutu. But, in fact, this was all window dressing and the real power in Rwanda now lay with Kagame.

I took a break from this story. I had to. It has been almost a month since I wrote the previous section.

I was forced to come to terms with the fact that remembering Rwanda was not going to be easy. After I returned to Eritrea, I had nightmares for weeks. I know that was true for many others I worked with in Kigali.

I remember greeting a new arrival at the embassy one day with a handshake and the quip, "Welcome to hell."

Hell was exactly what it was. Most people cannot imagine the absolute horror of what happened in Rwanda, and in this they are blessed, but probably it is most difficult for Americans to do it. We have been too long at peace in our own homes to know what it is like for genocide to strike in our own backyard. In Europe, they did experience the Holocaust within living memory.

There are things you can see that you can never un-see. There are things you can know that you can never un-know. Like staring at the Medusa, which legend has it will turn you to stone, it is dangerous to look complete evil in its face, and the reality of Rwanda and what I saw was complete evil.

The pause in my writing this was to prepare myself to walk through that door again and call back the demons of Rwanda I locked away. In the end, I found telling this story is probably one of the reasons why I am writing it.

What follows is a short summary of the facts about the Rwandan genocide.[1]

Rwanda has a population of about eight million and is divided into two main tribal groups, the Tutsi and the Hutu. Tutsi cattle herders began arriving in the area in about the fifteenth century and gradually subjugated the Hutu inhabitants. The Tutsis established a monarchy headed by a king and a feudal hierarchy of Tutsi nobles and gentry, reducing the Hutu to virtual serfdom.

However, boundaries of race and class blurred over the centuries through intermarriage, and the status of many Tutsi nobles declined until most Tutsis enjoyed few advantages over the Hutus. In 1899, the Tutsi king allowed the territory to become a German protectorate. Belgian troops from Zaire chased the Germans out of Rwanda in 1915 and took control of the country.

After World War I, the League of Nations placed Rwanda and its southern neighbor, Burundi, under the jurisdiction of Belgium as the territory of Ruanda-Urundi. Following World War II, Ruanda-Urundi became a U.N. Trust Territory with Belgium as the administrative authority. Reforms instituted by the Belgians in the 1950s encouraged the

---

1. Some of this synopsis is taken from State Department reports on the history of Rwanda.

growth of democratic political institutions, but Tutsi traditionalists who saw them as a threat to Tutsi rule resisted them. An increasingly restive Hutu population sparked a revolt in 1959, resulting in the overthrow of the Tutsi monarchy.

During the 1959 revolt and its aftermath, hundreds of thousands of Tutsis were killed or fled to neighboring countries. The new Hutu-based government was granted internal autonomy by Belgium on January 1, 1962. A June 1962 U.N. General Assembly resolution terminated the Belgian trusteeship and granted full independence to Rwanda effective July 1, 1962.

Inefficiency and corruption began festering in government ministries in the mid-1960s. On July 5, 1973, the military took power and dissolved the National Assembly and the ruling party and abolished all political activity.

In 1975, Juvénal Habyarimana formed the National Revolutionary Movement for Development (MRND). Rwandans went to the polls in 1978, overwhelmingly endorsed a new constitution, and confirmed Habyarimana as president. President Habyarimana was re-elected in 1983 and again in 1988, when he was the sole candidate. Responding to public pressure for political reform, he announced in July 1990 his intention to transform Rwanda's one-party state into a multi-party democracy.

On October 1, 1990, Rwandan exiles, primarily Tutsis whose parents had fled the country in 1959, banded together as the Rwandan Patriotic Front (RPF) and invaded Rwanda from their base in neighboring Uganda. The rebel force blamed the government for failing to democratize and resolve the problems of some 500,000 Tutsi refugees living in Diaspora around the world. The war dragged on for almost two years until a cease-fire was signed July 12, 1992, fixing a timetable for an end to the fighting. Political talks to establish some form of power-sharing began on August 10, 1992.

On April 6, 1994, an airplane carrying President Habyarimana and the president of Burundi was shot down as it prepared to land at Kigali. Both presidents were killed. Instantly, military and militia groups began killing all ethnic Tutsis as well as all moderate political leaders, regardless of their ethnic background.

The prime minister and her ten Belgian bodyguards were among the first victims. The killing swiftly spread from Kigali to all corners of the country, and between April 6 and the beginning of July, a genocide of unprecedented swiftness left up to one million Tutsis and moderate Hutus dead at the hands of organized bands of militia called *Interahamwe*. Ordinary citizens were ordered by local officials and government-sponsored radio stations to kill their Tutsi neighbors, and they did. The dead president's party was believed to have been behind the organization of the genocide.

The rebel Tutsi army resumed fighting, and civil war raged concurrently with the genocide for two months. The Rwandan Army was quickly defeated by the rebel Tutsis and fled across the border to Zaire, followed by some two million Hutu refugees who feared Tutsi reprisals for the genocide. The Tutsi rebels took Kigali on July 4, 1994, and the war ended on July 16. The rebels took control of a country ravaged by war and genocide.

Now you know the sad history, but not what really happened or why, or the monstrous evil behind it all.

CHAPTER 13

The distinction between Tutsis and Hutus in Rwanda is largely mythical, both tribes living side by side for so long that they share the same religion and language. Since they have intermarried for centuries, what your father is determines to what tribal group you belong, no matter how much blood you have from the other side.

In short, ethnic differences became a tool of manipulation rather than the reflection of any differences between people, religion, or culture. It is said that Tutsis are taller and thinner, while Hutus are supposedly squatter and broader. However, widespread exceptions make the rule pointless.

So why did these people fall to killing each other with such brutal abandon?

In a country as poor as Rwanda, the primary path to wealth and prestige lay in achieving political power and not through business or farming or other means of production. Governments in countries like Rwanda are largely unrestrained by the rule of law and any system of checks and balances. The ruling elites control a rubber-stamp legislature (when one exists at all), and the courts lack independence. Judges do what they are told, or suffer the consequences. Those in power are almost entirely free to plunder the country's treasury.

For the Hutu elites who ruled Rwanda, their livelihoods and the security of their families depended on maintaining their positions of authority. There was no private sector they could safely return to because there was nothing to protect their businesses from being pillaged by the new elite. The courts and police responded to the interests of those in power, not the interests of the country or the rule of law.

It is not that exploitation is unknown in the United States, but not at this catastrophic level of dysfunction.

This was the situation in Rwanda, where a narrow ruling class controlled the country and its resources for their own benefit.

Enter the well-meaning West, including the U.S., and our determination to bring the benefits of democracy to the world. It is a noble and ambitious objective, but it is often true that the path to hell is paved with good intentions. Never was this truer than in Rwanda.

Enormous international pressure was brought to bear on the Rwandan government to end its monopoly on power, hold free, fair and transparent elections, and allow for power-sharing with the Tutsi rebels in order to end the war.

President Habyarimana reluctantly agreed to new elections and power-sharing. Accords were signed and promises made. A great deal of backslapping and self-righteous self-satisfaction went on among Western diplomats, the United States included.

It was an agreement the government never intended to implement; at least, not considerable parts of the government. They were buying time. What they did with that time was to organize militia in almost every community across the country. Also, they organized a system of radio stations that were nominally private, but which again were under the control of pro-government forces. In a very poor country like Rwanda, where illiteracy is high, radio is the most effective means of mass communication. Last, they drew up death lists of people to be eliminated.

All of this activity was organized around getting out the message: Hutus could never allow Tutsis back into the government. Tutsis could not be trusted. They had for centuries exploited Hutus, held them in virtual slavery, and their rule had only been ended by violence. If allowed back into the government, it would only be a matter of time before Hutus would be slaves again.

This was a cynical manipulation of Hutu fears. The overwhelming majority of Hutus were as oppressed by the ruling elites as the Tutsis. It is an old game practiced all too often by political parties. Divide the people against one another and divert their hate and frustration into fighting each other instead of focusing on what really afflicts them.

When the killing started, the death lists did not distinguish between Tutsi and Hutu, and Hutus who supported democratic change were murdered along with their Tutsi colleagues. Those in power were equal-opportunity killers. Was President Habyarimana in on the planning? It is hard to say, but I cannot image he was completely unaware of the extensive preparations underway. What I suspect is that he knew, but thought he could control what would happen. Genocide was his fallback ace in the hole. I also think that other members of his government began to fear he might go through with the democracy plan, and decided to act to prevent it.

In their own horrific way, they were clever. On April 6, 1994, Habyarimana was returning to Kigali when his plane was shot down on its approach to the airport. No one knows who fired the missile, but the government immediately accused the rebels. It was the excuse needed to start the genocide.

In less than twenty-four hours after the plane went down, the killing started. At the beginning, it was well organized, going after specific targets who were all opponents of the government or who supported compromise with the rebels, both Hutu and Tutsi. It stretches credibility to think that this was spontaneous and unplanned.

The government, as a confidence-building measure with the Tutsi rebels prior to completing a power-sharing agreement, had allowed a unit of the rebel army to be garrisoned in Kigali. The rebels were taken by surprise when the killing started, and had to fight their way out of the capital. While the rebel leadership might have been willing to risk sacrificing these men after assassinating the president, it seems unlikely they would have put them there if shooting down the plane had been their plan.

While the killing was not, at first, random, it quickly grew in scope. Radio stations across the country went on the air calling for Hutus to murder all Tutsis. The militias began the killings, but many willing participants quickly joined them. The militias also took note of those who did not join in, killing them to incentivize others to join the slaughter in a cascading wave of death and brutality. There were documented cases of religious leaders, I am sad to say, gleefully encouraging the slaughter. There were things done to children and infants that I will not describe, they are so bestial. People who had lived next to each other for years turned on their neighbors with a viciousness that is difficult to fathom.

It is significant that in several accounts I read, as the mobs did their butchering, they chanted, "Insects! Insects!"

The Americans (many of them with the U.S. military) who went in and discovered these mutilated bodies had to go into counseling to deal with their nightmares.

In talking to people in Kigali, I was told that in the city it was more difficult for Tutsis to be identified outside of their neighborhoods. In the countryside, as you would expect, everyone knew everyone else, and when the killing started it was thorough. Many believe that one million people died in less than three months, and the majority killed were murdered up close and personal with knives and machetes.

The awful irony of all this organized murder is that, in the end, the authors of it did not achieve their goal. Quite the opposite. At the outbreak of the killing, the rebels resumed their offensive. Government troops, losing discipline in their orgy of civilian extermination, were quickly routed by the Tutsi rebel forces, who became highly motivated by the slaughter of their relatives throughout Rwanda. General Paul Kagame, who it is universally acknowledged was a brilliant strategist in carrying out the war, also led them. Within three months, the government collapsed and fled the country.

In the end, everyone lost everything there was to lose.

But in this sad country, that was not the end of the tragedy.

The fact remained that many, if not most, of the Hutu population had participated in the killing. They feared, as a result, Tutsi retribution. Even those who did not kill feared they would be blamed and suffer the consequences. Millions fled into neighboring countries.

The world then witnessed the heartbreaking spectacle of poverty-stricken peasants carrying their few belongings on their heads in massive columns of fleeing humanity that stretched for miles, all headed to countries that lacked the infrastructure, food, staff and funds to receive and assist them.

The result was predicable. Families were separated, young children lost, and the weak and elderly died on the roads. The new refugee camps overwhelmed donor country capacity to deal with them.

The camps themselves became death traps. Without access to sanitation and adequate drinking water, cholera and other water borne diseases ran wild. In the camp in Goma, Zaire, it is estimated that up to 10,000 people died every day at the height of the epidemic. The bodies piled up like cordwood.

Even the earth worked against them. The terrain around Goma is composed of volcanic rock, and bulldozers could not dig mass graves in the hard subsoil fast enough to get the dead into the ground, so the exposed corpses further propelled the spread of cholera.

Again, all this tells you is the numbers, not what it was like to be there. Kigali had been a city of 500,000 people. When I arrived, I doubt there were more than 20,000. It was, quite literally, a ghost town. I walked down empty streets past empty homes and shops, the road littered with the cast-off debris of broken lives and lost hopes. Shades of the murdered sulked in doorways and stared down from behind dark windows. No Stephen King novel can begin to approach the depth of the horror that was Rwanda in that summer of 1994. It would haunt my dreams for months to come. Its icy grip has never fully left me.

This kind of horror and instability feeds on itself. The moment I arrived in Kigali, I understood that we had to do everything we could to bring the refugees back. Those huge camps of frightened and displaced people were breeding grounds for future instability. We knew that large numbers of militia and government troops, the very people who organized the massacres, were also in the camps and still armed. Under international law, they were not supposed to be in the camps at all, but there was no one who could disarm or keep them out. It was obvious to me that these elements were going to take over the camps and recruit new soldiers from among the dislocated to continue the fight against the new government in Kigali.

The U.S. army has what are known as Psychological Operations Units, or PSYOPS, who immediately approached me. They had the resources to establish radio stations in Rwanda and along its borders to broadcast messages to try and get people to leave the camps and come home. Paul Kagame, the new leader of Rwanda, understood, I believe, the danger these camps posed to his country, and he said he wanted the refugees to come home. There would be no massacre. I believed him.

I thought we needed to get this program moving immediately, and went to the ambassador to get his approval.

He was horrified. Under no circumstances, he said, were we to do anything to encourage the refugees to return. If there were murders, and he was sure vengeful Tutsis would murder Hutu refugees, then the United States would be blamed. We would have blood on our hands.

That we already had blood on our hands for forcing the elections that resulted in the genocide, and for not doing enough to stop the killing when it began, haunted him, I believe. He could not bear the thought of more people dying through U.S. actions.

This ambassador was a good man, who had grown up in the region as the son of missionary parents, and he spoke the local languages. He loved the local people and he desperately wanted to help them, and he was exactly the wrong person for the job. He was distraught, and had gone through far too much to be back in charge of the embassy. The State Department should have anticipated this and should never have sent him back. Further, his experience of growing up in the region had taught him, I think, to distrust the Tutsi faction in this conflict because of their past history of political domination. Now that the Tutsis were back in control in Rwanda, he feared they would stage a massacre of Hutus. He was wrong in this, as subsequent events were to show. Not that the new government was to be free of human rights abuses, far from it, but not on the level the ambassador predicted.

In Rwanda, we had negotiated a peace deal that supposedly established a more open government with free and fair elections, and the State Department leadership never saw the need to convince the local population of the benefits of what a more open political process would mean to them. The result was that the elite leadership of the government party was able to manipulate public perceptions to create a massacre and destroy our democratic plan.

The people of Rwanda, just as with the people of Iraq, must want democracy and understand and support its principles and the institutions that underpin it before democracy can take hold. This means such things as respect for the rule of law, even when you disagree with the outcome; tolerance for political dissent; an understanding of the role of the media as the watchdog of good governance; and, most important, the development of stable institutions of government that are respected by the people. None of these existed in Rwanda.

Which brings me back to his misplaced priorities concerning getting the refugees home. Tens of thousands were already dying of disease in the camps, camps that were rapidly falling under the control of the very militias that had organized the genocide in Rwanda.

The opportunity to try and turn them around passed. The militias did recruit from the camps. Not only did the militias begin to attack Rwanda again, but the presence of these large refugee camps fatally inflamed ethnic tensions in Zaire itself. The instability that resulted from these conflicts across the border inside of Zaire exploded into a continent-wide conflict that saw armies from across Africa sent into Zaire to take sides in the struggle, most of them spending far more time raping Zaire of whatever natural resources they could steal than in fighting to suppress the civil war this conflict ignited. (Note: Zaire has subsequently been renamed Congo).

We had a flag-raising ceremony at the embassy to officially mark its reopening, and CNN International reporters broadcast it on television. In the report, I could be clearly seen standing near the flagpole. My wife saw the segment on television, and it was the first real news she had of me, since the phone lines were down in Kigali and I had no way of contacting her. Friends at the embassy in Asmara also saw it, and they remarked to my wife that I looked good.

She shook her head. "Something's wrong," she said. "He's not happy at all. It's going badly there."

CHAPTER 14

I present here a dilemma I have observed, concerning the laws of unintended consequences, that has me confounded. Across the developing world we run aid programs that have met the very laudable goal of reducing infant mortality and maternal death resulting from childbirth. We have spent tens of millions of dollars and done some astonishing things, such as completely eliminating smallpox. We are close to doing the same with polio. Effective and inexpensive vaccines are everywhere administered to countless children who would otherwise die or be crippled by disease. More vaccines are on the way, perhaps even one for malaria, one of the biggest killers in the developing world. It is nothing short of a miracle.

And yet the impact of these efforts could well be a legacy of war, famine, misery and the creation of new and even worse diseases.

The dilemma is that we are engaging with societies that do not have, in many cases, even the most basic healthcare infrastructure, and we are doing for them what they cannot do for themselves. But consider that when we do it, we are distorting the progress of those societies and often creating unstable social development that results in violence.

I pose a question. It is a shocking question, *and I do not have the answer*, but I pose it because I think it needs careful thought. The United Stated Agency for International Development, or USAID, prides itself on the fact that it can prove it has saved the lives of tens of thousands of women and children through its maternal health programs. But was it the right thing to do?

The great social philosopher and satiric writer, Jonathan Swift, pondered this question when he published his famous satiric essay, *A Modest Proposal*, an edited excerpt of which I present here:

> *It is a melancholy object to those who walk through this great town or travel in the country, when they see the streets, the roads, and cabin doors, crowded with beggars of the female sex, followed by three, four, or six children, all in rags and importuning every passenger for an alms. These mothers, instead of being able to work for their honest livelihood, are forced to employ all their time in strolling to beg sustenance for their helpless infants: who as they grow up either turn thieves for want of work, or leave their dear native country to fight for the Pretender in Spain, or sell themselves to the Barbadoes.*
>
> *I think it is agreed by all parties that this prodigious number of children in the arms, or on the backs, or at the heels of their mothers, and frequently of their fathers, is in the present deplorable state of the kingdom a very great additional grievance; and, therefore, whoever could find out a fair, cheap, and easy method of making these children sound, useful members of the commonwealth, would deserve so well of the public as to have his statue set up for a preserver of the nation.*
>
> *But my intention is very far from being confined to provide only for the children of professed beggars; it is of a much greater extent, and shall take in the whole number of infants at a certain age who are born of parents in effect as little able to support them as those who demand our charity in the streets.*
>
> *I shall now therefore humbly propose my own thoughts, which I hope will not be liable to the least objection.*
>
> *I have been assured by a very knowing American of my acquaintance in London, that a young healthy child well nursed is at a year old a most delicious, nourishing, and wholesome food, whether stewed, roasted, baked, or boiled; and I make no doubt that it will equally serve in a fricassee or a ragout.*
>
> *I have reckoned upon a medium that a child just born will weigh 12 pounds, and in a solar year, if tolerably nursed, increaseth to 28 pounds.*
>
> *I have already computed the charge of nursing a beggar's child (in which list I reckon all cottagers, laborers, and four-fifths of the farmers) to be about two shillings per annum, rags included; and I believe no gentleman would repine to give ten shillings for the carcass of a good fat child, which, as I have said, will make four dishes of excellent nutritive meat, when he hath only some particular friend or his own*

family to dine with him. Thus the squire will learn to be a good land-lord, and grow popular among his tenants; the mother will have eight shillings net profit, and be fit for work till she produces another child.

Some persons of a desponding spirit are in great concern about that vast number of poor people, who are aged, diseased, or maimed, and I have been desired to employ my thoughts what course may be taken to ease the nation of so grievous an encumbrance. But I am not in the least pain upon that matter, because it is very well known that they are every day dying and rotting by cold and famine, and filth and vermin, as fast as can be reasonably expected. And as to the young laborers, they are now in as hopeful a condition; they cannot get work, and consequently pine away for want of nourishment, to a degree that if at any time they are accidentally hired to common labor, they have not strength to perform it; and thus the country and themselves are happily delivered from the evils to come.

Therefore I repeat, let no man talk to me of these and the like expe-dients, 'till he hath at least some glympse of hope, that there will ever be some hearty and sincere attempt to put them into practice.

After all, I am not so violently bent upon my own opinion as to reject any offer proposed by wise men, which shall be found equally innocent, cheap, easy, and effectual. But before something of that kind shall be advanced in contradiction to my scheme, and offering a better, I desire the author or authors will be pleased maturely to consider two points. First, as things now stand, how they will be able to find food and raiment for an hundred thousand useless mouths and backs. And secondly, there being a round million of creatures in human figure throughout this kingdom, whose whole subsistence put into a common stock would leave them in debt two millions of pounds sterling, adding those who are beggars by profession to the bulk of farmers, cottagers, and laborers, with their wives and children who are beggars in effect: I desire those politicians who dislike my overture, and may perhaps be so bold as to attempt an answer, that they will first ask the parents of these mortals, whether they would not at this day think it a great happiness to have been sold for food, at a year old in the manner I prescribe, and thereby have avoided such a perpetual scene of misfortunes as they have since gone through by the oppression of landlords, the impossibility of paying rent without money or trade, the want of common sustenance, with neither house nor clothes to cover them from the inclemencies of the weather, and the most inevitable prospect of entailing the like or greater miseries upon their breed for ever.

I profess, in the sincerity of my heart, that I have not the least personal interest in endeavoring to promote this necessary work, having no other motive than the public good of my country, by advancing our trade, providing for infants, relieving the poor, and giving some pleasure to the rich. I have no children by which I can propose to get a single penny; the youngest being nine years old, and my wife past child-bearing.

Obviously, Swift did not seriously mean that the people of Ireland should sell their children for meat, but was making the point that eating them was, ironically, more humane than allowing them to suffer so extremely over the course of their hopeless lives. His argument, of course, was that his society needed to find a way to deal more effectively with rampant poverty. Simple handouts only made the situation worse.

We face, I think, a similar dilemma in our current development work around the world. When we go into societies that cannot now provide the basic services needed to support their citizens, are we really helping by saving lives that in the future cannot be sustained? Are children who are rescued from death by smallpox, only to grow up in crushing poverty, without education or opportunity or hope, really saved?

In Sierra Leone, where my adopted son is originally from, this very crushing poverty led many young men and boys to join a murderous rebellion that tore their society apart and, in the end, only further destroyed the infrastructure of the nation and its institutions.

I don't mean we should do less to help people. We should not do less; we should do more. We are a great nation, with great wealth and power. But we need to do a better job of it. Our record so far is not that encouraging; not for want of trying or noble purpose, but because most of the time we don't really know *how* to do it.

What we want to accomplish is great and worthy of us, but international aid is massively complicated, and is often made much less effective by shortsighted domestic politics, our incredibly short attention span, and by the American notion that we can fix everything and solve every problem. The result is an understandable frustration with how little we often achieve.

We should invest time, effort and money on better studying the issue. To do this, we ought to better fund international institutions entirely devoted to developing strategies that will work in helping poor countries to develop healthy and sustainable societies by creating holistic approaches to the problem. It does no good to deliver healthcare to mothers and children when the people saved are destined to grow up in hopeless environments that only foster the very violence and extremism we are fighting to end. How do we effectively give someone a boost who needs a boost and will benefit from it, verses doing for someone what they cannot do for themselves and therefore cannot sustain?

The first step is to end the paternalism of our aid programs. Paternalism would at least be justified if we could say that it helped, when in fact we so seldom do help.

President George Bush proposed an excellent model for how to start in his Millennium Challenge Account proposal. I would end USAID as we know it today and use the Millennium Challenge Account, or MCA, as a jumping-off point for restructuring aid programs.

The genius of the MCA is that it deals with something USAID is poorly equipped to handle, and whose institutional culture, in fact, resists confronting, which is that political, social and economic development all go hand-in-hand, and you cannot have one without the others.

The philosophy behind the MCA is that, instead of giving small amounts of money to a lot of countries, many of which may actually be adversely affected, we consolidate our funds and focus on those nations that have the social, political and economic capacity to support and nurture development. Those countries that meet such criteria, which have the capacity to benefit from a boost, would receive massive infusions of funding to help jump-start the process. This is what the Marshall Plan did in Europe after World War II with great success. The capacity for development existed in Europe, and we provided the funds required to get the engine started. There are other success stories: South Korea, for instance. Where we were successful, why? Where we failed, why? Study and use these models to chart future efforts.

The other benefit of this approach is that it treats the target country as a partner in the development process instead of as a dependent child. Partnerships work, dependency fails.

In countries where these conditions do not exist, we should not offer development assistance. We are wasting our time. An example is Zimbabwe. The former president of Zimbabwe, Robert Mugabe, was a madman and he ruled a country that, under his authority, was destroying itself. Nothing we could do was going to prevent that. In addition, I have little confidence that the opposition movement in Zimbabwe will make a significant change in the country's direction now that Mugabe is out of power. I do not think that even humanitarian assistance has been of much use in Zimbabwe, since Mugabe did all he could to block its distribution to the most needy and rerouted it to his supporters to the extent he could. In the end, all we accomplished was extending the time that Mugabe could hang on to power, and thereby extended everyone's misery.

In cases like Zimbabwe, we should instead encourage and promote political evolution in the country while also understanding the limits of what outsiders can accomplish in such situations.

There is, of course, the "Iraq" solution of sending in outside forces, seizing control of the country and creating a new social order. But this approach is difficult, risky, seldom works and is expensive, while helping those who are ready, willing and able to help themselves is productive and creates good models for others to follow.

Of course, the trouble with the MCA was that although it was an excellent idea, it lacked proper implementation. President Bush never got the money for it that he proposed, and never made a serious attempt to pressure Congress to allocate the funds. I saw the project take shape while working in the State Department, and domestic political considerations began to creep into the selection of countries to receive the money, further undermining the concept. Nations received money based on political preferences instead of on who would make the best use of the funds.

It is too bad. It was a good idea whose time has come.

CHAPTER 15

My assignment to Rwanda lasted a month. First and foremost, I did my job the best I could. A top priority was finding Rwandan employees of the embassy who were alive and putting them back to work. They needed and wanted to work because it kept their minds off of what had happened to them. They also needed the money to start rebuilding their lives.

I also had presswork to do. The local press was, to all intents and purposes, out of service, but I had plenty of international reporters to deal with, all looking for official U.S.G. comments and reactions to events. I arranged a number of interviews with the ambassador.

We had a regular parade of official and VIP visitors, most of whom came to shake their heads sadly on camera in front of American reporters.

I walked into my office one morning to discover a man who looked remarkably like the Reverend Al Sharpton sitting casually next to my desk. He was with three other men, one of whom immediately jumped up and stuck a video camera in my face, demanding, "What's your name and who are you?"

Since this was my office, it seemed more like the kind of question I should have been asking him.

Amused rather than intimidated, I told them I was the Public Affairs Officer at the embassy, and I gave my name. I then asked who they were and what they wanted.

I was told the man sitting before me was, in fact, the Reverend Al Sharpton.

I have to admit that this was just about the last person I expected to meet when I got up that morning. I was also going to have to talk to my staff about letting people into my office without telling me.

I asked the Reverend Sharpton what I could do for him.

Before he could answer, one of his hangers-on replied that he was on an important fact-finding mission, they had just arrived from Goma in Zaire, and the Reverend Sharpton needed a helicopter to take him back to Zaire.

I apologized and explained that I did not have a helicopter to lend him. The embassy had no helicopters.

"Are you refusing to assist Reverend Sharpton?" I was pointedly asked, the camera again shoved in my face.

No, I explained, I was happy to render whatever assistance I could to the Reverend, but I could not give what I did not have.

In his defense, Reverend Sharpton seemed annoyed by his aggressive colleagues, and he politely began discussing with me what he might do to get back quickly to Zaire. I suggested he go to the airport and speak to the U.S. military commanders out there. I provided him with some contact names, but said I had not seen any helicopters in use by them since my arrival, although they did sometimes fly transport planes to Zaire to supply our military helping out there, and he might be able to catch a ride if they had anything going in that direction today.

I took them out to the airport but, as I had suspected, the U.S. military had nothing going to Zaire that day. In the end, they got in their all-terrain vehicle and headed back to Goma by car.

For transportation in Rwanda, we used the old embassy vehicles that had surprisingly not been touched during the looting. Several local guard employees of the embassy continued to work at their jobs, even though no Americans were there and they did not know if they would ever be paid, and it was entirely due to their efforts that the embassy was saved from being ransacked during the genocide. The problem with the cars was that no one could find the keys, so I had to hotwire a station wagon allocated to my section. My favorite moment was driving the ambassador to an official meeting and reaching under the dashboard to connect the proper wires to get the car started. The ends of the wires were all bare, and the ambassador was concerned that I might electrocute myself. I assured him I was perfectly safe.

Foreign Service officers need to be versatile.

The embassy was staffed by a number of American officers, including U.S. Agency for International Development folks who were there to get assistance flowing to starving refugees. There were also State Department officers who had been serving when the embassy was originally evacuated. All of them were scarred by what they had been through, and they should never have been allowed to return. One officer, while the genocide was in full swing, had been on the phone with a desperate local employee calling her from his home. As she talked to him, she heard a mob break into his home, and then his screams as they killed him.

The State Department is very poor at handling its people when they have been traumatized by unspeakable events, and Rwanda was about as unspeakable as it gets. So we had many people hanging on to their sanity by a thread. It made us a close-knit group, and we often socialized in the evenings to talk and be supportive. In particular, I remember one Friday evening in the basement of the embassy. We were gathered in the old medical unit, and someone brought a bottle of Jack Daniels. We did not have glasses, however, and were not sure how to share the whiskey until someone found the stool specimen cups. They were perfect, since they had a wax lining to keep any sloppy stool from leaking out, and they held the whiskey just fine. We all got drunk, laughed, ate U.S. army-issued rations called MREs (meals ready to eat) and had a good time.

They were good people to work with if you had to be in hell.

After a few weeks, someone was sent in to relieve me and I returned to Eritrea.

CHAPTER 16

After Eritrea, I returned to our headquarters in Washington to become a country affairs officer in our Near East/South Asia (NEA) office. I was the "desk officer," as it is called, for public diplomacy in Israel, West Bank/Gaza, Jordan, Syria and Lebanon. This was in 1996.

One perk of being a desk officer was traveling once a year to the region I covered. It gave me a chance to visit the offices I supported in the field and see the problems they faced firsthand.

We had a public diplomacy office in our embassy in Beirut, Lebanon. However, the security situation there was so precarious that the number of Americans permitted to work at the embassy was strictly limited, and no American officer managed the public diplomacy office, only local staff.

There was a problem, however. The Lebanese staff constantly bickered, the Deputy Chief of Mission at the embassy was threatening to fire them, and it was felt an American public diplomacy officer needed to look into fixing things. They sent me.

This was in 1997, and things have changed since then, but at that time the only way to get to our embassy in Beirut was to fly to Cyprus and catch a ride on a U.S. military Blackhawk helicopter. The schedule of the Blackhawks was a closely guarded secret, so I arrived in Cyprus a day before the flight and could tell no one where I was going. If you compromised any of this information, the flight was scraped. We didn't want terrorists to know when the choppers were flying into the embassy so they could attack them.

The Blackhawks always flew in pairs so if one was hit, the other could attempt a rescue. We wore bright orange "Gumby" survival suits covering us from head to toe. In the event of a water landing, the suit kept us from dying of hypothermia, as would happen within fifteen minutes without them.

We put on the survival suits and it was true: with the hood on, I looked like a fair approximation of an orange Gumby.

We rode with the cargo door open and an armed guard positioned there to watch for people or boats to shoot at, should they prove hostile. With the door open, the engine roar was deafening.

When we reached the embassy, the choppers hovered three feet off the ground so that they could leave in an instant if fired upon.

I was quickly and efficiently ushered around the helipad, and then the Blackhawks were gone, and in the odd quiet that followed an hour and a half of hammering engine noise, I found myself in Lebanon.

CHAPTER 17

The embassy sits on a hilltop above Beirut commanding a picturesque view of the Mediterranean, Beirut being spread out in a narrow band along the coast. The embassy compound is twenty-five acres surrounded by tall fences crowned with razor wire. In all directions, guard towers watch over open fields, and any approach on foot or in a vehicle can be clearly observed by heavily armed guards. Many of the embassy buildings at that time had a curious metal frame hung around them, draped with what resembled thick chicken wire. Their purpose was to catch rocket-propelled grenades and mortar rounds and cause them to explode before penetrating the buildings.

Off compound, security was even more dramatic. On appointments for my job I traveled in a heavily armored car with six armed bodyguards and a driver trained to evade ambushes. When we stopped, my bodyguards jumped from the car, guns drawn, each facing in a different direction. When I entered an elevator, two came in with me, and the other four raced up the stairs and were always waiting for me when the doors opened.

And this was nothing compared to how Ambassador Richard Jones traveled. It was a tough job, and my hat was off to Ambassador Jones. He was an effective diplomat, gracious and good-natured, in a hard and dangerous job. And if he had not invited me to dinner and poisoned me with spoiled shrimp, I would say even more good things about him. On the plus side, I lost ten pounds.

When I traveled with him, we moved in a convoy of eight armored cars and trucks. Two trucks carried fifty-caliber machine guns mounted on swivel turrets that the guards constantly rotated, surveying passing buildings and terrain for threats. Other guards with machine guns hung out the windows of the vehicles.

These vehicles stopped for nothing. Not traffic lights, not traffic jams, not anything. Sirens blaring, we went through or around it all, and God help you if you got in the way.

We did not have Marine guards at that time, as is usual with most embassies. The Marines thought it was too dangerous. The bodyguards protecting us in Beirut were not Americans, but Maronite Christians, experienced killers who had fought in the Lebanese civil war for one or another of the Christian militias, and who favored the American presence in Lebanon.

For six weeks I had appointments with university officials, artists, past exchange participants, government officials and others. I fixed the conflicts between our Lebanese staff and put the office in good working order, and then I went home.

CHAPTER 18

In 2004, the biggest natural disaster of our lifetime struck when an underwater earthquake created tidal waves that swept through Southern Asia and as far west as Africa.

A friend of mine worked at our embassy in Bangkok, Thailand, and described what happened there:

"I was about as far from the low-lying beach as one could be when the earthquake hit. I know exactly where I was and what I was doing because I was scared stiff as I dashed over the rippling, swaying floors of my apartment on the 26th floor, the entire building swaying back and forth, out of sync with neighboring skyscrapers, for a full five minutes, the structure groaning, creaking and cracking in a background of threatening silence.

"It went on and on. The guy next door had a heart attack. But people on the ground in Bangkok barely noticed.

"The tsunamis did hit Thailand hard, but world attention to the damage and death here is exacerbated by the higher proportion of western tourists affected.

"But all is a bit chaotic as I wrestle with memories of other disaster relief and evacuations I've worked, like Tiananmen Square in China, or, with particular pain, meetings on the logistics of dealing with 10,000 bloated, decomposing bodies floating into Lake Victoria during the Hutu genocide in Rwanda.

"Tense and uneven time, like any crisis. Have to remember to be grateful I was not, in fact, on the beach."

This disaster will be remembered for two things: first, the monumental devastation and loss of life, and second, the incompetence with which the Bush Administration handled it.

When 9/11 struck and 3,000 Americans died, the world stood aghast and sympathy poured in from concerned world leaders. The death toll from this tsunami disaster eventually reached over 227,000 in eleven countries.

This was an opportunity for the United States to change our highly negative image in the world during the Bush Administration due to worldwide opposition to the war in Iraq. It could have been our finest moment.

President Bush should have immediately flown back from vacation in Texas to convene his Cabinet and outline our response. He should have called leaders of the other major donor countries to discuss how best to coordinate the rescue efforts. Then the president, Don Rumsfeld and Colin Powell should have appeared together to announce to the world our recognition of the enormity of the tragedy, our sorrow for the families of its victims and our commitment to do whatever was required to aid those in need. Powell should have outlined our diplomatic efforts to coordinate a response, and Rumsfeld should have announced that all American military resources we could muster were on their way to the region to assist survivors. Especially important would be the deployment of C-130 transport planes to carry supplies, as well as helicopters to deliver those supplies to communities isolated by the destruction and in desperate need of help.

This was the plan I sent to State Department leaders in the aftermath of the disaster.

The problem we faced was the absence of the involvement of President Bush. His initial response that we would render "all appropriate aid" was not well phrased.

We spent many billions of dollars in Iraq on a failed policy that resulted in the deaths of tens of thousands of Iraqis. Bush should have immediately said we would commit a billion dollars in aid to cope with this disaster, and that we would provide more later, if it proved necessary.

Many of the communities affected were Muslim, and the Muslim world thinks that we hate them and do not care about their welfare, and this was our chance to demonstrate for all to see the truth. It would have gone a long way in repairing our international image.

Instead, the president sat isolated on his ranch in Texas, "clearing brush and riding his bicycle." He did not make a public statement until four days after the event, and even then he did it from his ranch. Other world leaders cut short similar vacations to show leadership.

Meanwhile, Colin Powell's State Department was equally wretched in its handling of the crisis, focusing on the pathetically small amounts of money we were pledging, allowing us to be placed on the defensive when reporters pointed out the obvious fact that much more was going to be needed.

And Don Rumsfeld was nowhere to be seen.

The damage was done. This is why one U.N. official publicly called us stingy in our response, and that is what will be remembered even if it is not true. Perception is everything, and even though, in the end, we did make significant contributions, and more than anyone else, we did not get the credit for it. Instead of reacting immediately, our delay, our uncoordinated responses, but mainly and most importantly the absence of presidential leadership, again trashed the American image in the world when just the opposite could have been accomplished.

The importance of effective public diplomacy cannot be overstated.

Ronald Reagan is credited by many with winning the Cold War through his dramatic expansion of the U.S. military. However, the prospect of assured mutual destruction through the use of nuclear weapons kept both sides in a military stalemate. There was never a military win.

Ronald Reagan did do something significant to win the Cold War, and for which he is never credited: he dramatically increased the budget of a little-known federal organization called the United States Information Agency, or USIA, the public diplomacy arm of our struggle against Communism.

The Cold War was won by the power of ideas, and USIA was the lead Cold Warrior in the Soviet/U.S. clash of ideologies. Almost every American embassy in the world hosted an American Cultural Center that included popular libraries, people-to-people exchanges geared to influencing up-and-coming local leaders, university-to-university partnerships including the Fulbright and Humphrey fellowships and speaker and arts programs featuring prominent American academics, business leaders, politicians and artists. The Voice of America was another valuable influencer of foreign public opinion. As the world information revolution made it increasingly difficult for totalitarian regimes to control what its citizens heard and read, USIA took advantage of that to reach larger audiences behind the Iron Curtain. That Ronald Reagan understood the power of this kind of messaging was no accident. He was an actor.

The Soviet Union collapsed because its people lost faith in Communism. We won because we had the better ideas, and because our values of free expression and personal liberty, among others, converted world opinion. USIA was the little federal agency that played a major role in making that happen.

When the Cold War ended, some termed it "the end of history." Senator Jesse Helms of North Carolina, and others, said the United States no longer needed USIA to defend our values, tell our story and to counter Russian disinformation. He was instrumental in abolishing it. Ronald Reagan was no longer president to defend it, and many of its functions were poorly and ineffectively absorbed into the State Department.

The end of the Cold War was not the end of history.

Today we face a new enemy and a revitalized old one without the tools to most effectively confront them. We are largely treating the War on Terror as a military conflict instead of an ideological battle, and the Russians are humiliating us not with their military might, but through hacking and social media. Even after we take back all the territory ISIS holds in Iraq and Syria, much as we did to al-Qaeda in Afghanistan, we cannot defeat them until we have discredited their ideological allure. As we see in Afghanistan, al-Qaeda has risen from its ashes and is again a threat to the government in Kabul, and the continuing bloody attacks in Europe and elsewhere show the resilience of the appeal of radical Islamic fascism. As for the Russians, never has a country so humiliated us at so little cost through tools that ought to be our strength, not theirs. In the effort to win the social media struggle, we are coming in last.

Winning this war of ideologies ought to be a cakewalk. On our side we have freedom of expression, freedom of worship, education, tolerance, prosperity and the prospect of peace. On their side is the ruthless suppression of human rights, the brutalization of women, intolerance of other views, poverty, endless war that is doomed to failure in the long run and an ideology of hate and division.

The State Department is seldom credited with how much it has done to project American power to keep us safe. It is staffed with some of the best and brightest our country has to offer. It is excellent at government-to-government negotiations, creating treaties and promoting American business interests. What it is not good at is people-to-people diplomacy. It is not a part of the corporate culture of the Department and is essentially alien to its methods of operation, which primarily involve behind-closed-door negotiations and press conferences. Too often, press conferences are what leaders in the Department think is public diplomacy.

Public diplomacy is about establishing relationships between foreign audiences and Americans. Often, it has little to do with directly advocating foreign policy goals and is more about creating common ground even when we disagree about specific issues. It is about developing alliances and partnerships with foreign publics and leaders.

It is also about nurturing democratic development through promoting the evolution of institutions that support the rule of law. Democracy is a fragile form of government, as our Founding Fathers understood. The Electoral College was originally established as a potential check on what they feared might become mob rule by the majority. Originally, the electors were not required to vote for the person who received the most votes in their state. Senators were originally appointed until as late as 1911, not elected, and every state was given two no matter its size, again partly as a check on a majority gone mad. It was also a way to give Southern states more power to protect slavery.

Despite all this, in 1860 the democratic election of Abraham Lincoln sparked a bloody war that killed over 625,000 Americans. That is the level of violence elections all too often ignite, and did, even in our own country.

It is time we abandon the belief that elections make a democracy. Elections do not make democracies; they are the outcome of democracies. By promoting elections in countries without democratic cultures, we consistently put this cart before the horse with disastrous consequences.

There are societies and cultures that, in their present state, are incompatible with democratic governance.

It takes time to build the foundational elements of democracy in cultures where they do not exist, and it is a complex task that requires a long-term commitment of people and resources. We cannot mandate democratic change as we attempted to do in Rwanda, and we cannot install democratic governments without understanding the long-term commitment needed to push for incremental change. Democracies are never born in a matter of days or months with the stroke of a pen on an internationally negotiated treaty or agreement. Or with a gun.

One of George W. Bush's fiercest criticisms of the Clinton Administration when he ran for his first term against Al Gore was that the United States should not be in the business of nation-building, as Clinton had done with some success in the Balkans and very little success in Haiti. He then went on in Iraq to attempt the largest nation-building campaign since the reconstruction of Japan after World War II. The disaster of Iraq is a monument to the wisdom of not attempting it.

The fact is, we are miserably inept at nation-building because we understand so poorly what is required to do it right. It is never easy, and the correct formula for doing it is never the same. Every society is different, with different traditions, cultural norms and sets of base institutions from which to start.

Furthermore, the Bush Administration repeatedly pronounced its goal to bring democracy to the Middle East. The trouble was, they did not mean it.

In 2006, for instance, we saw the spectacle of Hamas winning a democratic election in the Palestinian Authority, and the Administration responded that we would have nothing to do with that democratically elected government until it changed its low-down ways. President Bush was right to do so, but it revealed him to be a hypocrite. He did not really mean he wanted democracies in the Middle East. What he wanted was for the people of the Middle East to elect the leaders we wanted them to elect. There are many more examples of this. Algeria in 1992. Iran in 1952. Chile in 1971. And on and on.

We simply do not have a clear idea of what it takes to bring about constructive and peaceful democratic development. In societies that have only known repression, are dangerously polarized ethnically, religiously and/or politically and which do not have in place the established and respected cultural, social and legal institutions needed to peacefully manage change, then suddenly unleashing the power of the people can result in violent social upheaval. All we often accomplish is to tear apart the very fabric of a nation we are trying to help. Societies are living organisms. You cannot, as we did in Iraq, tear off the head of that organism, transplant a new head onto it, and then be surprised to find that you have created a Frankenstein's monster.

We should work for democratic change, but just as with development aid, we need to be humbler about what is possible and a great deal smarter about what we are doing before we wind up killing more people in our ham-handed attempts to bring them the benefits of our system of governance.

We must understand better how to bring about change in ways that create self-reinforcing positive feedback loops. Our obsession with holding elections and then walking away congratulating ourselves on a job well done is devastating.

In September of 1999, I went to Senegal in West Africa where I was the Public Affairs Officer at our embassy in Dakar working with one of my favorite ambassadors, Harriet Elam-Thomas. Senegal was remarkable for its activist media, especially in the developing world.

Senegal did not always have an activist print media, and had only created an independent radio system around the time I arrived. That open media environment exists today, at least in part, due to the work of U.S. Public Affairs officers over two decades. Early on, they recognized the potential for media liberalization in Senegal and began to send journalists, editors and government officials on short- and long-term journalism study tours in the U.S. They brought media and democratization experts to Senegal to give lectures and hold conferences. Brick by brick, year by year, they planned and worked to build a new media environment in Senegal, believing that an independent media, one that could hold the government accountable, was a key leverage point to creating the means to achieve democratic reform.

Senegal, in September of 1999, was approaching a presidential election. The question for the embassy was, how could we support free, fair and transparent elections? Because of our long history in promoting journalism, and the growing institutional strength of that media, we decided to work with the Print, Radio and Television Journalists Federation to hold a series of workshops on the role of journalists in covering elections. The most popular lecture during the conference concerned new technologies, with a focus on the use of cell phones to provide breaking news, and the journalists used what they learned. In one instance, a radio reporter found a politician from the ruling party openly buying votes. He called his radio station and they put him on the air, live. He walked straight up to the man, identified him, asked him what he was doing and shoved the cell phone in his face. The man stuttered a few words, then turned and ran from the scene, to the laughter of all.

It caught on. Reporters everywhere went looking for cases of voter fraud to expose. On election night, all of Senegal stood by their radios. The results were to be sent to a central vote collection point in Dakar, where the government supposedly would confirm the tallies before announcing results. But reporters were announcing the totals, precinct by precinct. People kept their own tallies on scraps of paper and, by the next morning, everyone knew who the winner was, and for the first time in the history of the country it was not the incumbent.

Of course, one advantage we had in Senegal was that it simply wasn't much on Washington's radar, with little White House or Congressional interest. Left alone, the public diplomacy office and a series of ambassadors in Senegal over the years created an effective program that didn't cost very much. Sadly, our foreign policy is often heavily dependent on domestic policy, budgets and U.S. politics that frequently get in the way of effective long-term strategies.

USIA was uniquely organized to promote democratic development through the evolutionary promotion of human rights organizations, journalism, programs that helped build the rule of law, through education programs that encouraged the acceptance of diversity in society and more. It worked over decades to set the foundations that must be established before democracy can flourish.

This was the role of public diplomacy as USIA practiced it. We need its approach and tools if we are to defeat the terrorist ideology, counter Russian disinformation and fake news and build democracies without igniting violence.

CHAPTER 19

In 1998, I was offered a one-year Congressional Fellowship program intended to provide members of Congress with exposure to Foreign Service Officers and vice versa. The U.S. military has had similar and extremely effective programs like this for many years.

It works well for both sides. A senator or representative gets a free staffer for up to a year (the State Department still paid my salary), and we got experience working on the Hill and a chance to educate the Hill on what we do and why.

The problem is that Congress really does, on the whole, despise the State Department. That is, admittedly, partly the fault of the Department. The administration officials who staff the senior ranks of the Department generally feel they report to the White House and Members of Congress should steer clear of foreign policy concerns, an executive branch responsibility. I remember one hearing I attended when a congressman excoriated Madeline Albright because he had sent a letter to the State Department requesting information on a program, and after six months had still not received a response. Secretary Albright did not seem concerned about it, which further infuriated the congressman.

I spent a couple of months assembling my resume and visiting offices on the Hill, offering my services. I went equally to Republican and Democratic offices. Because of the hostility many in Congress feel toward the State Department, my reception was sometimes cold. For instance, Jessie Helms was notorious for his invective against the State Department, and I applied to work in his office. I thought it would be interesting and provide his staff with an insider's point of view that they might find useful, if not instructive.

They never even bothered to answer my letter or messages.

I eventually wound up meeting and working for Congressman Steven Rothman, a Democrat representing northern New Jersey. At the time, Congressman Rothman was on the House International Relations Committee (called the HIRC) and the Judiciary Committee. He thought my foreign affairs expertise would be useful in his work on the HIRC.

I was fortunate. Steve, as he insisted his staff call him, was one of the most decent members of Congress I met, and it was a pleasure working for him. His staff, on the whole, was typical of the Hill. Most of them were young, much younger than me, and worked for fairly low salaries. His chief of staff, however, was older, more experienced and better paid, as was typically the case.

It is not widely known outside of Washington that kids barely out of their teens essentially run our national government. They are energetic, thrilled to be at the center of legislative power, will work long hours without complaint and for low wages no one else would accept, and they make up the majority of the staffs of most senators, congressmen and congresswomen.

Members of Congress typically deal with more issues and votes than they can possibly keep track of. Mammoth bills are introduced with little or no advance notice and without the time needed to give them a thorough evaluation, let alone even a quick read.

So many legislators are heavily dependent on these young staffers to tell them what is in a bill and how they should vote. Usually, these kids also write the bills. That is how, for instance, it was discovered that a large bill that included language on the Internal Revenue Service was found to have sections in it allowing two Members of Congress free access to any citizen's tax return. The congressmen named claimed to have no knowledge of these sections of the bill, and denied that they wrote them.

Two of their staffers owned up to writing the sections, and it is possible the congressmen did not know about it. Paying close attention is a lot of work, diverting them from the Capitol Hill pastime of fundraising and sniping at the opposition.

This was not true of Steve Rothman, who did rely on his staff for advice, but who also kept abreast, to a large extent, of the issues before him and how he should vote.

Congressman Rothman's office was short on space, with his core staff all housed in a single room. I had a desk and computer in a corner. Steve had one person, a young fellow named Raffi, dedicated to dealing with international affairs issues for his work on the HIRC. Being Jewish, and serving an area with a sizable Jewish community, Steve took a special interest in Middle Eastern affairs. When I came on board, Steve gave Raffi the Middle East, and I was assigned the rest of the world.

It was a fascinating time to be on the Hill. The crisis in Kosovo was brewing and I became Steve's expert on the War Powers Act that supposedly sets limits on what a president can do with the U.S. military without a declaration of war from Congress.

The impeachment trial of President Clinton was also just starting in the Senate.

In addition, Steve had a sizable Irish American constituency and I worked extensively on the situation in Northern Ireland, even drafting a piece of legislation.

I wrote several speeches and got to watch Steve deliver them, although he used his staff-written material only as a guide and made many modifications on the fly.

I attended scores of meetings with other congressional staff, coordinated with Senate offices on a host of issues, and contributed to strategy sessions dealing with passing legislation. I sat behind Steve during HIRC meetings and fed him questions when various members of the Clinton Administration testified before the committee, including Madeline Albright.

Groups interested in proposing, supporting, or opposing legislation were constantly hosting events. I could pretty much skip dinner every evening if I wanted because someone was always putting on a feed to attract congressional staff. The food was great and there was always plenty of anything you wanted to drink, from Jack Daniels to Coke. I remember one event, in particular, by the ice cream industry where lunch was any flavor of ice cream I wanted.

The Capitol has an impressive underground transportation system, including small trains and subway-like cars connecting all the buildings on Capitol Hill. It was easy to get lost, and several times I did.

I met nearly all the political leaders you saw on television at that time, including all the Republican Members of Congress conducting the prosecution of Bill Clinton.

In short, I loved it.

I was very enthusiastic when President Clinton nominated Madeline Albright to be Secretary of State. I thought we were getting a smart and accomplished woman who would be a strong leader capable of working effectively with Congress. However, looking back over the last fifty years, I would rate Madeline Albright and Rex Tillerson the worst Secretaries of State of my lifetime.

Albright's greatest failure was her mishandling of the Kosovo crisis.

Kosovo was a part of the disaster involving the breakup of the former Yugoslavia, another example of a reasonably prosperous people ripping apart the very fabric of their society over trivial ethnic differences that no one in his or her right mind would ever consider important enough to kill over, let alone murder, rape, pillage and "ethnically cleanse" at a rate in Europe not seen since World War II.

Yet that is what happened. Yugoslavian President Slobodan Milosevic, who eventually went on trial in The Hague for war crimes, promoted "ethnic cleansing" (such an antiseptic label for mass murder) of unruly fellow citizens in an attempt to preserve Serbian dominance in Yugoslavia. In the end, all that his brutality achieved was the continuing loss of territory to competing ethnic groups who, through his atrocities, were provided with increasing motivation and support to resist his reign of terror.

Kosovo was a province in southern Serbia with a majority Albanian population. The more Milosevic repressed that population, the more resentment he created, until large-scale violence broke out in February of 1998. In October of 1998, U.S. envoy Richard Holbrooke brokered an agreement with Milosevic that achieved a brief pause in the fighting. He essentially did it through the threat of unleashing NATO air strikes on Serbia if it did not stop killing people.

A January 1999 massacre of forty-five ethnic Albanian civilians in the village of Racak, including women and children, ended the cease-fire.

By this time, about 2,000 mainly ethnic Albanians had been killed and about 350,000 became refugees. Increasingly, the Kosovars were flocking to the support of the Kosovo Liberation Army, or KLA, whose goal was to create an ethnic Albanian state independent of Serbia (and who were also responsible for plenty of their own ethnic violence against the Serbs). The more Milosevic attacked the Kosovar Albanians, the stronger the KLA grew. While the majority in Kosovo would originally have accepted some kind of compromise settlement that recognized Albanian rights within Serbia, Milosevic was driving them into the arms of the extremist KLA.

Madeline Albright decided enough was enough. She considered Milosevic a schoolyard bully, and the way you take on schoolyard bullies is to stand up to them. She was impatient with the hesitation of our NATO allies to get tough, not to mention our own inaction for too many years in the face of Milosevic's butchery.

It was not that she was wrong. She was right. It took us far too long to put an end to ethnic cleansing in the former Yugoslavia. Tens of thousands of people died in the heart of "civilized" Europe while NATO, the U.S. included, did little more than wring our hands.

In Yugoslavia there were things we could have done to help end the fighting. These actions wouldn't have posed a risk to us, our chances for success were high, and we occupied the moral high ground. Admittedly, our national interest in ending the killing in Yugoslavia was not compelling because America was not threatened, but in the face of genocide we ought to do something if we can and if what we do helps.

The problem was how badly Albright mishandled the whole affair, which cost many lives.

Admittedly, it is easy to sit in judgment on leaders like Madeline Albright, who are, after all, only human and make mistakes like the rest of us.

But when you lead the policy apparatus of the most powerful nation on Earth, lives hang in the balance. Albright needed to proceed vigorously, yet cautiously, constantly checking on conditions and questioning assumptions to be sure that the outcomes she wanted were the outcomes she would get.

Albright pushed for a conference to take place in Rambouillet, France, in early February of 1999. The supposed objective was to negotiate an acceptable accord between the Kosovar Albanians and the Serbs that would end the fighting. Albright developed a "peace plan" that she intended to impose on Milosevic. He would be forced to accept it or face the threat of NATO bombardment.

But there were problems. First, she developed her plan without talking enough to the parties involved. She did not care what Milosevic felt or wanted, and she assumed that the KLA, representing the Albanians, would embrace her proposal. It was a mistake.

Her plan called for the establishment of new political institutions and offices in Kosovo, free elections and human rights guarantees. A NATO military force would ensure compliance, and the accords provided NATO with the right to enter Serbia and go wherever it wished (a clear slap in the face to Milosevic) to insure implementation and to provide a secure environment. The United States pledged to contribute troops to a NATO-led peacekeeping force. However, and this is a big however, Kosovo would not achieve independence from Serbia.

As one of Congressman Steve Rothman's legislative aides, I attended several foreign policy planning meetings, including, when the conflict in Kosovo began to boil over, meetings with members of the KLA in Washington. It was immediately clear to me that the KLA would not sign any agreement that did not grant them independence from Serbia.

This was critical. The success of Albright's plan depended on a united front against Milosevic, backing him into a corner as the "bad guy" who would not sign the accord the international community and the Albanians all agreed upon.

There is really no excuse for Albright not anticipating that the KLA would baulk at signing her accord. Her plan depended upon it, and the KLA was making no secret of the fact that they were not about to sign on to any agreement that did not grant them independence.

But this took Albright by surprise at Rambouillet at the worst possible moment. Instead of forcing the hand of Milosevic, it gave him an out when the KLA also refused to sign, enabling Milosevic to shrug and say, "You see, how can I sign on to an accord that the Albanians will not accept?"

The conference collapsed, and Albright was to blame for not putting her ducks in a row before it started. Albright spent the next few weeks twisting the arm of the KLA until they finally did agree to sign the accord, something she should have done *before* Rambouillet.

Milosevic still refused to sign it. I think the fiasco at Rambouillet convinced him that Albright was incompetent and he could refuse her without consequence.

Another reason he could believe this was because of another serious mistake. In fairness to Albright, this was the mistake of President Clinton, but it was a mistake that she should have worked hard to prevent.

It was announced that while we would contribute troops to a peacekeeping mission, we would not send troops into a fight.

Even if true, you never let your opponent have this kind of information. It is like playing poker and telling everyone at the table, if any bet I make is raised by five dollars, I will fold. For Milosevic, it reinforced to him that he had no need to fear the U.S. or its determination to make him obey any accords. When push came to shove, we were not serious about making him do anything.

If we would not commit troops, how serious were we about bombing him? And even if we did bomb him, how long could we keep it up? A day or two? It did not look like we had the stomach for more.

Last, bombing without the use of coordinated ground forces has almost never proven to be an effective military tool. Air power nearly always needs to be used in conjunction with ground troops, and we had said we would not use ground troops in a fight.

So, in his mind, what did he have to fear by ignoring us? Conversely, capitulating to our demands would destroy him politically with the Serbians. Agreeing to allow NATO troops to wander wherever they liked in Serbia was to abandon Serbian sovereignty, a humiliation of the Serbian nation. Defying the U.S. was a political win for him domestically, while doing what we wanted became a loss for Milosevic with his own people. It was a no-brainer which way he would choose, which made his popularity with the Serbian people soar, and this was all Albright's doing.

When the KLA finally did sign on to the accord, and Milosevic refused it, Albright went to work forcing NATO to prepare for air strikes.

Since he was going to be bombed anyway, and not believing that the bombing would be effective or sustained, Milosevic did exactly what men with his twisted logic always do. He organized another massacre. He prepared his forces and sent them into Kosovo on another ethnic cleansing mission, this time to kill or force out of Kosovo its entire Albanian population. His own "final solution." Kosovo would be entirely Serbian, again making him a hero with his own people. He did not see a downside. And best of all, the political opposition to him in Serbia would be forced to back down in the face of the NATO bombing of Serbia, making him even stronger. Albright's incompetence had not only failed to stop ethnic cleansing, but she had actually made it an attractive option.

Serb forces did the best they could to carry out the massacres and push out the Albanians. In the end, thousands died and hundreds of thousands became refugees. NATO began the bombing, but it is impossible to stop ethnic cleansing from the air without troops on the ground.

Milosevic miscalculated our determination to continue the bombing, and it did not last for just a few days. It went on for eleven weeks and it was devastating to the Serbs, decimating the civilian infrastructure of their country while actually inflicting very little damage on the Serbian military, which became adept at hiding their forces and creating fake military targets for us to hit.

On June 5, 1999, Finnish President Martti Ahtisaari and former Russian Prime Minister Viktor Chernomyrdin brokered an agreement with Milosevic to end the war. It was not the Rambouillet agreement, but one with terms that Milosevic might well have agreed to before the war had Albright had the skill and insight to negotiate it.

It was a dark moment for American diplomacy. In the end, we got what we wanted, but hundreds of thousands suffered needlessly.

CHAPTER 20

In late September of 2001, I was assigned to be the Deputy Director in the Office of West African Affairs, one of six regional offices in the Bureau of African Affairs in the State Department.

The goal of the bureau was to bring peace to Africa where there was war, and undermine dictators who abused their people. We also tried to alleviate the suffering of poverty through aid programs, and worked to end the scourges of AIDS and malaria.

In April of 2002, I was sent to Sierra Leone in West Africa for a month. Due to the civil war, dependents were not allowed at post. Our ambassador, Peter Chaves, wanted to take a break to visit his family, and he needed someone to assume charge while he was gone.

Sierra Leone is a small country on the coast of West Africa about the size of South Carolina. It is home to at least twenty tribal groups and languages, and while there are more Muslims than Christians in the country, many people mix elements from both these religions with their traditional African spiritual beliefs. The culture is rich, fascinating and mysterious.

The country's eleven-year civil war was one of the most brutal of the twentieth century, including sexual violence against girls and women as well as the usual looting, murdering and kidnapping. Sometimes entire families were pulled from their homes and burned alive. But the most notorious and horrifying acts involved the widespread amputation of hands, arms, lips, legs, eyes and other parts of the body; even infants and the elderly were attacked in this way.

By April of 2002, the war was finally winding down. The rebels had put down their arms and formed a political party to contest the elections to be held in May of that year. The worst of the rebel leaders, for the most part, had been captured or were in hiding. The very worst of them still at large, Sam Bockarie (AKA General Mosquito) was, we knew, in neighboring Liberia.

Still, the country was unstable and only essential personnel staffed our embassy. It had been evacuated on several occasions during the war.

Normally, the deputy chief of mission would have taken over as Charge d'Affairs in the absence of the ambassador from post, but Peter had lost his DCM, so AF/W sent me out to take over for a month.

At the time, no regular airlines flew to Sierra Leone. In order to get there, I went to London to pick up a "charter" flight. It had a regular schedule to Freetown once or twice a week, but the plane belonged to a charter company not averse to taking risks, unlike most normal airlines, and it flew the route so long as it was profitable and a plane could land without drawing fire.

In all honesty, by the time I went it really was safe—for the most part.

Freetown has the potential to be a beautiful city. It stretches over a series of hills, most of them overlooking the ocean, and there are few tall buildings, giving it a rather pastoral look and feel, like one large extended village.

It showed, at that time, the scars of war. There were occasional burned-out buildings, and everywhere I saw signs of bullet and shrapnel damage to walls. But there were also plenty of signs of life and recovery.

In fact, I found Sierra Leone a beautiful country. With plenty of rain, the forests and farms were unusually green compared to other places I had seen in Africa, which tended toward the dried savannah of Senegal and Eritrea. It had natural resources in abundance, including arable land, rich coastal waters, rivers, diamonds, gold and other minerals. In short, it had the potential to be a paradise with plenty for all.

Instead, it was about as poor as a country can get, with a population traumatized by years of the most horrific brutality imaginable, the result of a colossal failure of leadership and governance. The rebels, many of whom were certifiably crazy, had much to answer for, but so did the previous national leaders who created conditions where murderous adventurism was a viable alternative to the grinding poverty of a desperate people robbed of their national patrimony by a thieving elite governing class. It reminded me of something Abraham Lincoln once said of a member of his Cabinet: "The only thing he wouldn't steal was a red hot stove." That had been the leadership of Sierra Leone.

I was given quarters in an apartment complex perched on a hill overlooking the city and the ocean. The view was stunning. Amenities included the usual U.S.G. issued furniture, a functioning kitchen and satellite TV with access to American Forces Recreational Television and some of the latest movie releases on video. I watched most of the HBO *Band of Brothers* World War II series.

The staff at the embassy, both American and Sierra Leonean, was dedicated and hardworking.

There was one popular nightclub called Paddy's. It was near the ocean and nothing more than a large thatched-roof pavilion open to the night air on all sides, with a central bar and a dance floor that included a spinning mirror disco ball reflecting flashing squares of light over the patrons.

The place reminded me of the bar in the first *Star Wars* movie where Luke Skywalker and Obi-Wan Kenobi meet Han Solo for the first time. Any kind of alien you could imagine was at Paddy's, including ambassadors, generals from the United Nations peacekeeping forces stationed there, businessmen, hustlers, pimps, prostitutes, journalists, humanitarian workers, tourists, artists and former rebel soldiers. You could tell the former rebels by the scarring on their faces. Drugs were freely used during combat, and men made incisions on their faces into which they rubbed drugs because it gave them a better high, but it also scarred them.

The beer flowed, the music blared and anyone could talk to anyone else because rank was not recognized at Paddy's.

On a few occasions, I had women explain in graphic detail the kind of companionship they could offer me for a modest fee. The first time, I explained that I was married. "So?" asked the woman. "What does that have to do with it?"

Realizing she had a point, after that I just thanked them but said I was not interested, which was more to the point. That, they accepted without question.

Sierra Leone, like many places in Africa but especially in West Africa, had a substantial Lebanese community. Many of the families, if not most, had lived in these countries for generations and held citizenship. Given the ferocity of the civil war and the havoc it inflicted on the economy, I was surprised at how many remained in Freetown.

The Lebanese often had strained relations with their African countrymen. While they usually held local citizenship, as mentioned, they also held on to their Lebanese citizenship as an escape hatch. They often needed it. Marriage outside of their Lebanese community was somewhat rare, and being very successful businessmen and women meant that they were experts at survival in difficult situations and were adept at spreading money around to corrupt governments upon whose favor they depended in order to conduct their business interests. This communalism, success and connection to the seats of power often made them unpopular with the average citizen.

They were sometimes accused of being parasites, a holdover of the colonial period and its foreign exploiters. Sometimes it was true, especially in the diamond trade where some Lebanese and other traders made large profits trading weapons for diamonds, a trade that caused unspeakable suffering.

Yet the majority, I found, had a real attachment to Sierra Leone. I met one Lebanese doctor who assured me that he had stayed even when the rebels overran the capital.

Rebels soldiers went house-to-house, robbing, raping and killing. When they came to his, they forced him outside and held guns to his head. Just when he thought he would die, a rebel stepped forward and told the men to let him go. Surprised, they asked why.

"Because," he answered, "this man saved my mother's life. She was dying, and he treated her for free."

The rebels left, and he was not molested again. He did not remember the man or his mother. It was one of those countless and, to him at the time, seemingly inconsequential acts of kindness that he had performed during his life, yet this one saved him.

It makes me wonder how many points we reach in our lives where we make decisions, seemingly insignificant at the moment, that later have far-reaching consequences on the future course of events. You can never know, and most of the time probably would not even remember if someone told you, but they happen, and it is a reason for treating every moment as if your life depended upon the decision you make or the action you take. It adds up over a lifetime, and although it may not stay the executioner's hand because death is the end of us all, it makes a difference about who you are, and what you can say about yourself.

For the first and, I expect, only time in my life, I had two helicopters at my complete disposal. Outside of Freetown there was no good way to get around on the ground, at least not quickly. The contract for the helicopters was with an American company, but an American company using Soviet helicopters flown by pilots from somewhere in Eastern Europe. Bulgarians, I believe. They did not speak much English. On the positive side, however, we did not crash even once.

These helicopters performed yeomen service. When needed, they delivered food to starving refugee camps. They evacuated people needing medical assistance. They were used to ferry government election officials to remote polling places for the upcoming election and delivered ballots so Sierra Leoneans could vote for the first time in years. I used them to inspect U.N. peacekeeping operations. They were, in effect, helping to put the country back together. Without them, we would have been stuck in Freetown with little means to help effect the changes needed to end the war and bring peace to the country.

I went on one election-related trip with members of the National Election Committee. We interviewed members of all the registered political parties to see if there were any complaints of harassment or other problems. This included members of the Revolutionary United Front, or RUF, the limb-hacking rebels who were now a political party.

I have almost always found evil wears a face like anyone else. These former rebel leaders, men who had done so many appalling things, looked no different from their neighbors. Well, maybe there was an intensity in their eyes, a hint of darkness, that I did not see in others. But it was no more than a hint, and might have been something I imagined because I was looking for it. I think I wanted to see a difference. I want evil to look and sound like Darth Vader. I want evil to wear a black cape so we know it when we see it. I want evil to have a sneer, to be immediately odious and ugly, like a diseased rat, so that we know to banish it. It is, sadly, not like that.

I used the helicopters to visit a Pakistani and then a Nigerian peacekeeping contingent. The U.S.G. pays a major share of the costs of peacekeeping operations in most places like this, so Washington wanted me to look to see we were getting our money's worth. In both places, I inspected the forces, got a rundown on their preparations for keeping the country secure during the upcoming elections, received briefings from commanders and their staffs and had lunch. With the Nigerians, I ate Nigerian food. With the Pakistanis, I ate South Asian food. I also always received a gift coffee mug bearing the insignia of the unit I was visiting as a memento.

At the embassy, I sat in the office of the Deputy Chief of Mission, or DCM. I did not want to disturb Peter's office. The only unusual feature of my office was a series of holes in the wall where a rocket-propelled grenade round had penetrated the room during a battle for the capital. The holes neatly lined up in a slightly climbing trajectory, ending in one pillar at the far end of the room. Since the last hole was about the size of the RPG round that made it, I concluded it was still embedded deep in the pillar.

Well, I thought, if it has not gone off after all this time, what were the odds on it exploding now? Besides, if it was still live, trying to pull it out was more likely to set it off than just leaving it.

I did accomplish one major feat of diplomatic dexterity. An important vote was pending involving a human rights committee in the U.N. and we wanted Sierra Leone to vote with us on the issue. We very much needed their vote, in this particular case, but it would require Sierra Leone to break ranks with other African nations on the issue, something that African leaders hate to do because they often then catch hell for supposedly being a puppet dancing to the tune of the United States.

I paid a visit to the Foreign Minister and laid out the issues for him. We had done a lot for Sierra Leone. We would do much more. But if Sierra Leone did not help us out from time to time on issues of importance to us, people would notice in Washington and it would become difficult to make the case that Sierra Leone was an ally. And, of course, of all the countries in the world, Sierra Leone ought to understand the importance of ending human rights abuses. Its people had suffered enough from them.

In the end, they helped us out.

There were other undertakings, the daily give-and-take of the art of diplomacy. My work in Sierra Leone was, for the most part, engaging. I met President Kabbah on several occasions, traveled around the country in my own helicopters, rubbed elbows with the elite and drank plenty of beer at Paddy's with the common man. American embassy employees stood up when I walked into a room and I oversaw the smooth functioning of an aid program that Americans can be proud of.

Peter came back and I was glad to go home again, but I did so with many good memories of an American mission well managed to good effect.

CHAPTER 21

After Sierra Leone, back in Washington I settled down into the routine of work in support of our embassies in West Africa.

And then events unfolded in Liberia that changed everything.

John Blaney was our ambassador to Liberia, a conflict zone where tours at our embassy were unaccompanied. John had been there several months, and two of his daughters were about to graduate from school. He wanted to be home for it, and he needed someone to come out to run the embassy while he was gone. This was in April of 2003, and I volunteered.

Liberia, which means "land of the free," was founded by freed slaves from the United States as part of a white-sponsored scheme to send all blacks in the U.S. back to Africa. Those freed slaves, called Americo-Liberians, established a settlement in 1820 in what is now Monrovia (named after U.S. President James Monroe).

On July 26, 1847, the Republic of Liberia declared its independence. For 133 years Liberia was a one-party state ruled by the former African-American freed slaves and their descendants, until April 12, 1980, when indigenous Liberian Master Sergeant Samuel K. Doe seized power in a coup d'état. Doe's forces executed President William R. Tolbert and several officials of his government.

In December 1989, a small band of rebels led by Doe's former procurement chief, Charles Taylor, invaded Liberia from neighboring Ivory Coast. Taylor and his National Patriotic Front rebels rapidly gained the support of Liberians because of the repressive nature of Samuel Doe's government. Barely six months after the rebels first attacked, they reached the outskirts of Monrovia.

Taylor's rebel group then splintered when one of his lieutenants, Prince Johnson, broke away. Johnson's forces set a trap that succeeded in capturing President Doe, who was brutally tortured over a three-day period, including having his nose, ears and testicles severed. The rebels filmed their handiwork and sold DVDs of it in the local markets.

The civil war in Liberia ground on until negotiations conducted by the United States, the United Nations, the Organization of African Unity and the Economic Community of West African States led to elections in 1997, with Charles Taylor and his National Patriotic Party emerging victorious. Taylor won by a large majority not because people liked him, but because Liberians feared a return to war if Taylor lost. His most famous campaign slogan was, "He killed my ma, he killed my pa, I'm voting for Taylor!"

For the next six years, the Taylor government neglected the country and bled it dry. Unemployment and illiteracy rose above 75%, with little to no investment in the country's infrastructure. Like a carrion-eating beetle, Taylor continued to devote himself to the only thing he was good at: personally profiting from the carnage of war, which he did by supplying arms to bordering rebel groups in exchange for diamonds, gold and other commodities raped from his neighbors. He supported the bloody Revolutionary United Front in nearby Sierra Leone, fomenting unrest and brutal excesses in the region. Taylor hoped, in this way, to eventually wrench control away from his neighbors over large tracts of their mineral-rich resources. His strategy eventually backfired, however, when adjacent states turned against him and supported his rebel enemies inside Liberia. By June of 2003, forces opposed to Taylor were fighting his army on the outskirts of Monrovia.

And that is the history of Liberia in a nutshell up to the time of my arrival to take over the embassy. It was in Liberia that I came closest to being killed in the line of duty on at least one occasion, and where I first had to deal with what it was to be a leader when life and death hang in the balance.

CHAPTER 22

I arrived in Monrovia on an early evening in late April of 2003. Robert's Field, as the airport is named, was at that time shabby and run-down even by developing world standards, but that was typical of the whole state of Liberia's infrastructure, which was nothing short of stunningly dilapidated after decades of civil war and government mismanagement, neglect and corruption.

In many countries in Africa, electricity is a sometime thing, and in most places I lived our homes had generators to provide power when the city grid failed.

In Liberia, there was no functioning electrical grid at all, and privately owned generators produced all power. Some people made a business of selling electricity to neighbors to help underwrite the high cost of imported fuel oil.

There was also no city waterworks. The embassy hauled in water in tanker trucks and stored it. Many local residents of Monrovia dug wells next to their homes. It was the only major metropolitan area in the world, let alone the capital of a country, where the water system had completely disintegrated.

The public schools did not function. There were some private schools, but they cost more money than most people could afford.

Medical facilities were also few, lacking in basic supplies, and mostly run by foreign charity organizations.

For telephones, everyone used cell phones, a great advance in Africa because they bypassed the usual government telephone monopolies, which were nearly always badly managed, inefficient and expensive. Sewage just got dumped wherever it was convenient.

On the trip from the airport to the embassy, we were waved through several checkpoints manned by well-armed young soldiers in all manner of dress, from military fatigues to tee shirts and jeans. We were waved through instead of extorted for money because our license plates clearly advertised that we were with the American embassy. Rank has its privileges even when it comes to corruption.

The drive itself was startling for what it revealed about Liberia. The country was green and we passed miles of farms, most run-down and decaying, but the land itself looked rich and potentially productive. I did notice that, unlike most places I had been in Africa, there were very few farm animals. Chickens, which usually wander everywhere in African villages, were almost entirely absent, as were sheep, goats and other livestock, including dogs.

I later learned this was due to constant predation on farmers by both government and rebel forces. You could say they lived off the fat of the land, except that there was no fat left. Marauding armies had robbed the country into bankruptcy.

The embassy occupied a large space on a promontory overlooking the Atlantic; the compound included the Chancery itself, housing for the American staff, additional office space, warehouse space, carpenter and metalworking shops, a small store with various food items and beverages including beer and liquor, a bar and cafeteria next to a small swimming pool, a large building housing our electrical generators, several water storage tanks, a volleyball court and, very importantly, a helicopter landing pad.

Razor wire topped a high wall enclosing the compound, with entrance provided in two places by heavily guarded iron gates. I went jogging most mornings, and it took me fifteen minutes to run the inner circumference of the compound. Interestingly, someone had brought chickens in, and although there were few on the outside, we had plenty of them in the embassy. No one had the heart to eat them, and they reproduced at a steady rate.

From the living room of the house I was assigned, I had a beautiful view of the ocean and a tall, lush mango tree. In the evenings I sat, listened to music and watched the Atlantic sunset.

I spent the next several days getting to know the American and Liberian staff, and meeting with John Blaney, the ambassador.

John was not sure he could leave. A new rebel group had recently emerged in eastern Liberia, crossing over from the border with Ivory Coast. This was the Movement for Democracy in Liberia, or MODEL, and although it was hard to get reliable news on what was happening outside of Monrovia, it appeared MODEL had scored some surprisingly quick military victories and captured two larger cities.

President Taylor's problems were rapidly multiplying, and they were very much of his own making. After winning the election to become the president of Liberia and finally achieving his life's ambition, instead of focusing on trying to do something productive and create a legacy beyond being a murdering thug, he continued his lowdown ways. I think it was all he knew how to do. He certainly showed no interest in promoting the peace and prosperity of his own people.

But now Taylor's past was coming back to haunt him as his neighbors either actively supported rebel insurgencies against him, or turned a blind eye to their operations across their borders.

Furthermore, Taylor's bad behavior had brought international sanctions down on Liberia, and it was illegal in the international community to sell him arms. This did not stop Taylor from buying weapons, but it forced him into the black market trade, which meant paying top dollar for what he needed. I think Americans would be shocked to understand the extent of the international arms trade, especially the black market in weapons. The result is that the world is flooded with guns. In Africa, just about anyone who wants a gun, for whatever reason, has one. They're cheap, and Africa is the National Rifle Association's vision of paradise.

Not only was MODEL, the new rebel force, making dramatic inroads against Taylor's forces, but his old adversary the LURD (Liberians United for Reconciliation and Democracy) were also showing signs of new activity. They were operating out of the northwest of Liberia, across the borders with Guinea and Sierra Leone, two countries that hated Taylor for all the grief and murder he had helped rain down on them.

Part of Taylor's dilemma was that he did not trust anyone, and for good reason. This especially included his own armed forces, which he knew only too well might turn against him. People like Taylor get into their positions of power over the bodies of those who stand in their way, quite literally stabbing a friend in the back when it furthered his ambitions. Having done it so many times to others, Taylor knew how easily it could happen to him. He was a cold-blooded killer who had allies, but no friends.

And so he intentionally kept his military commanders as weak and dependent on him as possible. That involved dividing the military into competing factions that were difficult to unite should anyone attempt a coup. As a result, in addition to the regular military, there were several militias. These groups not infrequently fell to fighting each other, especially when loot was involved, because another thing Taylor did, or rather did not do, was pay his troops on a regular basis, and some he did not pay at all.

Taylor therefore sanctioned what popularly became known as military "Pay Yourself" campaigns, in which troops routinely pillaged what they wanted from the exhausted civilian population. This was the reason I had seen so few farm animals on my trip into town from the airport.

In the short run it was smart of Taylor to fractionalize the military and allow them to loot their salaries, saving him a great deal of money. In the long run, it was utter stupidity. But that was Charles Taylor, a man who was clever but not smart.

The fragmentation of military command, the lack of pay and the constant pillaging of the civilian population created an armed mob rather than an army. The soldiers were far more motivated to abuse civilians than fight armed rebels capable of shooting back at them.

In addition, now that Taylor needed munitions for himself to fight his own rebels instead of trading arms for profit with neighboring insurgents, he was paying top dollar on the black market, quickly draining his resources.

Finally, money for arms meant fewer dollars to keep his top people loyal. The more Taylor looked like a losing bet, the faster his lieutenants might jump ship to either join the rebels or, just as likely, turn and kill him.

Certainly, what happened to former President Doe was never far from Taylor's mind.

As for John Blaney's dilemma about going home or staying, everything depended on what happened with the rebel advances. If Taylor's poorly disciplined troops collapsed, the situation could unravel very quickly indeed.

We had about a week and a half to wait and see. We sat tight and watched.

In the meantime, we also tried to learn more about the mysterious new rebel movement MODEL, which appeared to be threatening the eastern port town of Buchanan. Buchanan was critical to Taylor for two reasons. First, a major foreign timber company operated out of Buchanan, and this was one of the last large sources of foreign revenue left to Taylor. In exchange for allowing the company to rape the forests of Liberia, Taylor received millions of dollars. Without that money, he would quickly run out of funds needed to buy weapons.

Second, Buchanan was less than a half-day's drive from Monrovia, and the international airport, Robert's Field, sat between the two cities. MODEL's capture of the airport would cut off Taylor's most important route for importing arms. It might also trap him in Monrovia, where, if the capital fell, he might be captured. He had no illusions about his fate should the rebels get their hands on him.

We knew almost nothing about MODEL, but we had a name from a website of someone who purported to be a leader. I discovered he was living in the U.S. near, if I remember correctly, Philadelphia. I called him. He answered the phone. Sometimes, believe it or not, diplomacy works this way.

We had several conversations over the next few weeks, with me trying to establish who he was, what the organization of MODEL was, who was in charge and what their objectives were. It essentially came down to the following: he claimed he was in charge, but in fact MODEL was a loosely knit group of opportunistic factions opposed to Taylor and led by an assortment of cutthroats. Subsequent peace conferences that included representatives of MODEL amply demonstrated that no one in particular was really in charge, and commanders in the field seemed to do what they wanted with minimal coordination. Their objective was to depose Taylor and take over the government. They dressed that up with plenty of rhetoric about peace, restoring democracy, bringing justice to the people of Liberia and so on and so forth. The two things that really held them together, however, were the opportunity to loot and their hatred of Taylor.

Ambassador Blaney held several senior staff meetings in which we discussed the situation and established what are called "trip wires." Embassies do this to avoid what I call the "frog in the saucepan" phenomena. It is said that if you toss a frog into a saucepan of hot water, the frog will immediately jump out knowing the hot water will kill him.

If, on the other hand, you place the frog in a saucepan of cool water, and slowly heat it, the frog will stay in the water until it dies. The change in temperature is so gradual that the frog becomes accustomed to the heat and does not realize the danger when the water becomes too hot.

Embassies are frogs. Ambassadors are loath to downsize or, finally, shut down their own missions. The longer you sit in a crisis situation, the more that crisis becomes the new normal and, growing accustomed to it, you no longer realize the danger. On more than one occasion we have nearly lost embassies for this reason. Somalia was a classic example. When that country fell apart during the first Gulf War, our ambassador waited far too long to shut down. Fortunately, because of the war, we had sufficient helicopters and ships in the area to pull people out at the last minute, but in that case, hostile Somalis were climbing over the embassy walls just as the helicopters arrived. It was a near thing that should not have happened.

So we set out in advance what we would do, and when, should the situation continue to deteriorate. We determined that if MODEL were to threaten an attack on Buchanan (which would probably result in the closure of the airport, our primary means of exiting the country), we would drawdown the embassy to minimum levels.

Given the violent history of Liberia, there had been drawdowns before. However, we had never actually closed the embassy. Our presence there was a stabilizing force that had helped in the past to stop the bloodshed when fighting came to the capital. Further, from our talks with all the rebel groups, we knew they wanted our recognition if they were victorious against Taylor, and so the last thing they wanted was to attack our embassy. But we would have to see how things developed.

So we waited.

The situation stabilized. There were contradictory reports about MODEL, but their offensive seemed to have stalled, and they might even have lost ground. The rumor was that they were short on ammunition, and that Taylor might have struck some kind of deal with Ivory Coast to restrict MODEL's ability to re-supply itself across their border.

It looked like John could make the trip back to see his family after all. Before leaving, however, he decided to pay a call on President Taylor. He wanted to discuss with Taylor the situation, see what Taylor's mood was, and introduce me so that Taylor knew I would be running the embassy until John's return, in the event I had to contact him.

We made the trek over to the Presidential Palace on the afternoon of a hot, cloudless day. Protocol required we dress in the usual diplomatic attire, including suit coats and ties.

We were met at the front of the building by smiling men in suits and grim-faced men dressed in jeans and tee shirts holding automatic assault rifles. Instead of being led into the building, however, we were taken through it to the grounds behind the palace, a large open space overlooking the ocean surrounded by a concrete wall. Escorted to a pavilion, we were shown to our seats.

It was obvious Taylor wanted to make us sweat. The pavilion was, as least, covered, so we were not directly in the sun. The chairs were arranged in a U formation, with John and myself on one side, a place for Taylor's advisors opposite us and at the base of the U, and armed guards standing casually nearby.

John and I took our seats and waited, not too long, but long enough for Taylor to make a statement about who was in control. When he finally arrived, he brought his chief advisors in tow.

John introduced me and we shook hands.

Taylor was dressed in a khaki safari suit and he carried a walking stick and a briefcase. He set the briefcase down next to his chair, and we all sat. Several times during the course of the conversation he eyed me carefully, sizing me up. He was medium tall, and only slightly on the heavy side. Having spent years in the field leading an army, life was obviously on the softer side for him now, but he had not grown fat.

Most of all, he looked sly in the way that you expect an experienced street hood to look sly. He knew the score, he knew who we were and he was ready to play the game.

He also liked to talk. A lot. In the end, we were with him for two hours and of that, John and I collectively spoke for about ten to fifteen minutes.

Mostly, he talked at length about how unfairly he was being treated by the United States. He was the legitimately elected leader of Liberia, and the sanctions on Liberia were unjust. Liberia only wanted to defend itself against its enemies, and the arms embargo severely tied his hands. If a burglar comes into your home to steal your possessions and threaten your family, did you not have the right to defend yourself? Where was the justice in tying Liberia's hands?

John asked him about MODEL and what was happening on the eastern front.

Taylor sniffed that MODEL was nothing but a rag-tag band of bandits and thugs masquerading as rebels. They presented no threat, and his forces would defeat them in short order. They were finished.

John reminded the president that there were arms and travel sanctions on Liberia because of his meddling in his neighbor's wars.

Taylor denied meddling. He was the victim of false charges. "If you have proof of any wrongdoing, present it," he challenged us. He had, he claimed, been tried, convicted and sentenced in the court of public opinion by slander and without proof.

He exuded confidence. He projected the air of someone who is secure in his position, who believes the threats against him are minor and easily deflected and that he is the great leader of his nation.

It is so odd to be in the presence of men like Taylor. He caused unspeakable suffering, murder and pillaging, but he denied all of it with the wave of a hand and the casual challenge to present the proof. For every accusation made against him, he had an excuse or outright lie.

He was a simple man, he told us, but misunderstood, and his only ambition was to serve his country and then retire peacefully to his plantation to the north of Monrovia. He was planting coffee, he said, and he would raise coffee and pursue the pleasures of a gentleman farmer in his retirement.

He went on at some length about his selfless devotion to his country, and the injustices done to him by those who slandered him.

Then he gave us a sly look. "You know," he said, "there have been reports in the past that Sam Bockarie is in Liberia. If he was, I did not know about it, and he has most recently, I hear, been in Ivory Coast. But there are reports he has crossed the border and may be in Liberia."

Sam Bockarie was a Sierra Leonean who had been a commander in the Revolutionary United Front, or RUF, in the civil war in neighboring Sierra Leone. He was widely credited, if it can be called that, with beginning the practice of amputating the arms and legs of civilians in Sierra Leone as a means of punishing those suspected of supporting the government. It was rumored that Bockarie had studied at a school for revolutionaries run by Muammar Gaddafi in Libya, where he was taught that terrorizing civilians was the most effective means of controlling them. The Special Court that had been established in Sierra Leone after the war indicted him for war crimes, and we knew that he was in Liberia.

He was a good friend of Taylor's, who shielded him from arrest, consistently denying that Bockarie was in Liberia. It was another of those Taylor lies that he said with a straight face in front of people who, he knew, knew better. But again, when pushed, his response was, "Tell me where Bockarie is and I will arrest him. Prove he is here." Taylor loved that line about proving things.

The irony was, we knew Bockarie lived in a house not far from Monrovia with his wife and family. But if you said that, Taylor answered, "We looked there and didn't see him. You must be mistaken."

I saw an opportunity to play upon Taylor's "wounded and misunderstood" pride.

"Mr. President," I said, "as you know, many have accused you of harboring Sam Bockarie, and this has gravely damaged your reputation in the international community. You say you have not. If he is now in Liberia, and you turn him over to the Special Court in Sierra Leone, you can prove your detractors wrong and do much to show the international community that you are misunderstood and maligned."

He stared at me a long moment, and then changed the subject.

Taylor was up to something, we knew, or he would not have admitted Bockarie was in the country. The problem for Taylor was that Bockarie was becoming too hot to handle. During the war in Sierra Leone, Bockarie was a good business partner in the human misery trade, and Taylor made a great deal of money selling Bockarie arms for diamonds, but now the war was over and Bockarie's side had lost. The cash cow was dry.

Even worse, Bockarie had become mixed up in the new civil war in Ivory Coast. With new chances to loot in that formerly prosperous country, Bockerie and his Liberian and Sierra Leonean mercenaries could not let that opportunity slip away. There were plenty of reports of stolen cars and trucks loaded with stolen consumer goods streaming out of Ivory Coast into Liberia.

We did not know the details, but it seemed Bockarie had screwed up this profitable operation by coming into conflict with a local rebel commander. Bockarie ambushed and killed him, and then fled the country when the man's loyal troops came after him for revenge.

So that was strike one against Bockarie as far as Taylor was concerned. Additionally, the pressure was mounting on Taylor internationally to surrender Bockarie, and now that Taylor faced tough fighting in his own country, he could ill-afford to shield General Mosquito, as Bockarie was also called. Last, it is possible that Taylor had made some kind of promise to stop looting Ivory Coast in exchange for that country slowing down the supply lines to MODEL, making Bockarie a parasite without a host to feed off of except for Taylor himself, and he increasingly could not afford it.

I had now presented Taylor with an option that rid him of General Mosquito while enhancing his reputation on the international scene by sending him to the Special Court.

Except we all knew Taylor could not do that. Sam Bockarie knew too much about Taylor's support of the rebels in Sierra Leone, and he could implicate Taylor in several war crimes. Taylor feared that the Special Court might indict him, and Bockarie could supply them with all the information they needed to do it in exchange for some kind of deal on prison time. Under no circumstances was Taylor going to send Bockarie alive to Sierra Leone.

I was not sure if Taylor would take action, but if Taylor arrested Bockarie and he happened to be shot trying to escape, well, those things happened. The Special Court would get its man, albeit dead, and Taylor could say he was a law-abiding neighbor to Sierra Leone who did the right thing, sorry about him not being able to talk to you.

While talking with Taylor, refreshments arrived, including sodas and various snacks. This drew the attention of three huge ostriches that had free run of the compound. One of the birds was male, and the other two female. The male took an aggressive interest in our food, and came up behind Ambassador Blaney, where, being much taller than a man, he had an excellent view over John's shoulder of the snacks. The next thing John knew, the bird was trying to snatch them from him.

Ostriches can be dangerous, and a kick from one of their powerful legs can easily kill a man. The servers rushed forward and, waving large empty trays, tried to make the bird back off. The bird hissed at them, opening its wings in a display of aggression and dominance. He took a look at Taylor, who was also eating, and stepped closer to him. Taylor's bodyguards raised their guns, and I feared that this was going to end badly for all concerned. Not only was the bird about to be shot, but we were sitting next to the damn thing.

The bird backed off, and John and I breathed easier. Taylor never looked anything more than mildly amused.

Our conversation finally came to an end, and Taylor dismissed us, picking up his briefcase and leaving with his advisors.

I was to meet Taylor once more, and found him carrying the same brown bag. If you opened it, I am sure you would have found a million dollars in cash and a fully loaded pistol. Taylor was always prepared to be on the run.

A few days later, we got a call at the embassy from the government. Sam Bockarie had been apprehended, but was killed trying to escape. He was in a morgue in Monrovia. Did we want to see the body?

I chose not to go, although I wanted to. It was a bit like being in *The Twilight Zone*, in that Mosquito was responsible for horrible atrocities, including things that happened to my son who was adopted from Sierra Leone, and the inhumanity he represented had inspired me to write a novel, *The Demon Stone*, in which he is a main character. I killed him in my book, and now, possibly, I had helped do so in real life.

But it just got stranger. Although I did not go to see Mosquito, I sent one of my political officers to view the body.

He came back and confirmed that it was Bockarie, only he had not been shot. He had been beaten to death.

We think that happened because Mosquito promoted a legend about himself that he could not be killed with bullets. I think his executioners were afraid that if they shot him, he would not die but would come back after them. The only way to be sure he stayed dead, they thought, was to kill him without shooting him. So they beat him to death.

Although there are people in the world who desperately need killing, and Mosquito ranked somewhere near the top, execution is not a cause for celebration. I was glad that justice of a kind was done, and glad that the world was now without a man like Mosquito, but I would never say it made me joyful: to feel that would make me like Mosquito.

And then I learned the price of unanticipated consequences. A few weeks later, we heard that Bockarie was not the only person murdered. Taylor had his whole family slaughtered, including his wife and all of his children.

What is the price we are willing to pay to see justice done? How many should die to get at a monster? Admittedly, they were his children, but they were children nonetheless, and it was their father who was the monster. They had done no wrong. I did not kill them, but it is possible they died because of something I did.

This was just the very beginning of the dilemmas I was to face concerning unanticipated consequences, and the complexities of life as a leader when you have to make life-and-death decisions. For my childhood hero Green Lantern, the decisions were always clear, and the path righteous. That is what I wanted. I was discovering the hard way that I was no Green Lantern. I was just Chris Datta, public servant, caught in the middle of some of the worst people on the planet and trying to save as many innocent souls as I could.

CHAPTER 23

John Blaney left, and the last thing he did was make me promise not to close his embassy while he was gone. I gave him my word.

At first, things stayed quiet. I took a trip to the city of Buchanan to see if government forces, in fact, had the situation under control, and I gave a talk at a school. I was invited to Rotarian lunches and gave speeches. I met with government officials and oversaw the operation of the embassy. I held staff meetings and collected reports on the state of rebel advances. At first, there were none. In fact, as Taylor had said, MODEL seemed to be bogged down.

Everywhere I went Liberians wanted to know what America was going to do to help them. Everyone, from your average citizen to church leaders to government officials, wanted an American intervention. They did not want it for the same reasons, but they wanted it. Even the rebels wanted it. Taylor's people wanted it because, with American troops in Monrovia, the rebels would never be able to attack the capital and Taylor could hang on using us as a shield. The rebels wanted it because they assumed we would arrest Taylor. Your average citizen wanted it because they were sick of the fighting and thought of America as a country that would stand up against oppression and bring peace and stability to their lives.

My response was always the same. We will help you, but you must help yourselves. The U.S. cannot make your country right if Liberians are not willing to make sacrifices and work out their differences. I often told the story of the man who prayed every day to God to let him win the lottery. He was good, he was honest, and he promised God he would do good deeds with the money. Day after day he prayed, and yet his prayer was never answered. One day, in exasperation, the man cried out to God, "Why, oh why, Lord, won't you let me win the lottery? What must I do?"

And the voice of God answered him, "Meet me halfway. Buy a ticket."

I said the Liberians had to meet us halfway and work for peace. It was not something we could hand to them, and if we tried, the peace would not last because it was not earned.

Life settled into a kind of normalcy. I particularly looked forward to Wednesday evenings, when the embassy Marines hosted a movie night at the Marine house. Any American could come, as well as foreigners escorted by an American. The evenings started off in the bar at the Marine House, where we drank beer and played pool. A group of American Roman-Catholic nuns always came. They ran a small hospital in Monrovia, one of the few still functioning. The head nun, a roundish woman in her fifties, was one kick-ass pool shark and she always shellacked the young Marines, to their constant humiliation. When they lost, they had to buy her a beer. They paid for a lot of beer.

I saw several movies, but only remember one: *Catch Me If You Can*. It was an ironic choice given we were in a war zone.

There was not a lot to do besides work, and we worked weekends. Another routine I developed was lunch at the embassy's open-air snack bar on Saturdays. I went jogging every morning, which took me by the ambassador's residence. I peered into a window I passed, looking at a portrait of the first president of Liberia. It was said to be haunted, and Ambassador Blaney once sheepishly told me that he often did hear eerie sounds at night coming from that room.

So life was good until it changed.

What changed was that the rebel group, Liberians United for Reconciliation and Democracy, or LURD, became active again. Guinea and Sierra Leone, neighbors to the north and west of Liberia, were backing the LURD to punish Taylor for supporting rebels in their countries.

It soon became obvious that LURD forces were, in fact, on the move, and this seemed to stimulate MODEL to increase activity. The race for Monrovia was on.

My nightmare scenario was for MODEL to come up the east coast, closing the airport, and for LURD to come down from the north, squeezing Taylor from two directions, until they both arrived at the outskirts of Monrovia with Taylor trapped inside with us. If that happened, there was an excellent chance everyone would wind up fighting everyone else in a competitive bloodbath to determine who would become the next Lord of the Flies. Certainly, little would be left of Monrovia when they were done slugging it out.

I met with my senior staff to discuss next steps. The situation was, on the whole, still under control, but it would stay that way only if Taylor's forces could hold. They had done so in the past, but might not this time around.

Up to that point, the official travel guidance of the State Department was that Americans should avoid travel to Liberia. We did not recommend, at least not officially, that Americans in Liberia should leave the country. We decided the time had come to do so. If MODEL closed in on the airport and it shut, our options for getting people out would be few. We had no U.S. military assets close at hand, and contrary to ridiculous reports in the local media, we had no large nuclear-powered submarine docked out of sight at the embassy.

We drafted a new consular message for Liberia, again warning Americans against travel to the country, but this time also urging Americans in Liberia to leave. The situation, we warned, was deteriorating and might suddenly collapse.

John Blaney kept in touch with me via e-mail, and he urged me to try to get a handle on the number of Americans in the country in case of an evacuation. An evacuation using what resources, I did not know, but he was right. We estimated there were about 500 American citizens in the country, but we did not know for certain. Finding out was a formidable problem. Phones, except for cell phones, did not work. There was no mail service.

However, we had established what we called a "Warden Net" of American volunteers in the community who could reach out to U.S. citizens. Each Warden was issued a two-way radio so we could communicate with them reliably, and each was asked to keep a list of Americans they knew in their area.

We activated the Warden Net, asking that all Americans register with the embassy so that we knew where they were and how to reach them. We also ran ads in newspapers and on the radio.

Some people did get the message and came to us.

The majority of Americans still in the country were dual U.S./Liberian citizens. Many were children born in the U.S., automatically making them citizens, but whose parents were Liberian. Most of the rest were missionaries or employees of relief groups. Liberia did not get many tourists.

The fighting with LURD forces in the north appeared to intensify as May went by. Despite our warnings, few Americans seemed to leave, however. Quite the contrary, more people kept arriving.

I received a call one afternoon from my Consular Section. A group of twenty-five newly arrived Americans were there to register with us. Most of them were college students, male and female, led by five adults. They were part of a missionary group arriving to work in an orphanage to the north of Monrovia, which might soon be in harm's way. The group was oblivious to the warnings of my Consular Officer, and I was asked to come down to try to talk sense into them.

The kids looked nervous. The adult attitudes ranged from curious to hostile. It was amazing to me that adults would bring twenty college kids into a country that their own government had warmed them to keep clear of because of the potential for getting their heads shot off.

I welcomed them to the embassy and thanked them for checking in with us. I read our consular warning, and briefed them on the potential for civil conflict. It was, I told them, my personal opinion that the situation was going to get worse, and that I had to recommend for their own safety that they leave. We were telling everyone to leave.

I explained that government forces were as much a threat to them, and perhaps more so, than the rebels. All the combatants were poorly trained, ill disciplined and eager to rob anyone they could.

The kids now looked scared, as did some of the adults. However, a couple of them glowered at me, defiant.

They were, one said, devout Christians there to do the Lord's work. The orphanage would need them more than ever if there was fighting, and Jesus would protect them.

My personal reaction was mixed. On the one hand, I respected their desire to help helpless children, who are always the principal victims of these wars. The children could, God knew, use all the help they could get.

On the other hand, I wondered if the parents of these college students were really aware of the danger their sons and daughters faced in Liberia. I doubted it.

I had met people like this before, brave and cavalier about taking risks until the threat was on top of them, and then screaming like newborns for help, with their relatives calling Members of Congress demanding to know what the American embassy was going to do to rescue their loved ones, and why it was not doing so already.

If the fighting came to Monrovia, and I was convinced it would, and twenty-five Americans found themselves trapped at an orphanage, I knew the pressure I would be under to send people out to try and rescue them. I had two diplomatic security officers, seven Marines, about 100 Liberian unarmed guards, and an American contractor who hired and trained the local guard force (he was an ex-Marine, so at least I could depend on him to know how to handle himself in a tight spot). There were potentially thousands of rebel and government soldiers, and I had an embassy compound I had to keep secure and not enough U.S. servicemen to do it.

The only two guys I could really send into a situation like that were my two diplomatic security officers. They were both married with families back in the States.

I explained this to the group, and told them that while I admired their desire to be of help to orphans, and I respected their faith in God, if they made the decision against my advice to leave and they found themselves trapped by the fighting, I would not risk the lives of the people I commanded to go to their aid. It would not be fair to their families to risk their lives when this group had, with full knowledge of the danger, made the decision to proceed.

It was a bluff, because I knew I could never leave twenty misguided and misled American kids in harm's way, but I wanted them to think seriously about what they were doing.

They conferred, and then the adults announced that they were staying.

I told them to keep in touch with us so that, in the event of an evacuation, we would know where to find them.

They would not leave the children, they said. God would protect them. But they did, at least, promise to stay in touch.

CHAPTER 24

Tensions in Monrovia were on the rise, and everyone looked to the American Embassy for answers or reassurance. For all practical purposes, I was the head of the last Western embassy left in the country. The French had two resident diplomats in town, but not an embassy. The European Community had a few people present, as did the U.N. The Egyptians and Chinese still had embassies, but that was it. I was in constant contact with them all, and they all wanted to know the American action plan.

The plan was simple. I had almost no cards in my hand to play. I had no U.S. forces nearby and, most troubling of all, no helicopters. If the airport shut down, I would be trapped.

Everyone wanted an assurance that, if it came to an attack on the city, I would take their citizens out on U.S. military helicopters. The U.S. in past evacuations had carried out the Lebanese community, which numbered in the thousands. They wanted to hear that I would do it again.

I could not do it, I told them.

They were shocked. Why not?

Because, I said, there are no helicopters. I had nothing.

But you are the Americans. You are the superpower. You can do anything.

Not here, I said. Not in Africa. Read my lips. Send your people out while they can still go, because if push comes to shove in Monrovia, I have nothing. I do not know how I will get myself out.

No one believed it. Often, they looked at me slyly and said, in effect, OK, what's the American game, really? What do you have up your sleeve? You are saying this to somehow put pressure on Taylor, right? You can tell us.

No games, I told them.

Stunned, they often protested: "But what is your Africa policy? Charles Taylor is a bigger killer than Saddam Hussein."

And all I could say was, "We'll do what we can, but as you know, we have big problems to deal with elsewhere."

The truth was, the Administration had no coherent Africa policy, but I could not say that.

Some of Taylor's senior people were also contacting me. It was intentionally left unclear whether they were talking to me with or without Taylor's knowledge. I generally assumed it was with, because to do it without was a dangerous game. If Taylor found out, the consequences could be fatal. But by pretending to be acting independently, Taylor could use them to probe us to try and discover what we were up to and what proposals from him we would accept or reject.

While Taylor had said to us, and had publicly proclaimed, that he was the rightfully elected president of Liberia, with a constitutional responsibility to remain in power until the end of his term, I was beginning to detect some give in that position based on what his advisors were telling me.

With the rebels on the move, Taylor was thinking of Former President Doe and his last day, mutilated and slowly bleeding to death. If the rebels won, Taylor needed a way out, and he knew it. Clearly, he was carefully weighing his options. He would do all he could to hold on, but he did not want to die if defeated. Taylor was, first and foremost, a survivor.

I knew Taylor would never leave unless forced to by rebel advances. That meant that the fighting had to come to Monrovia, or Taylor would not budge. John Blaney's top priority was to stop the fighting (and killing) while also backing the creation of a new government in Liberia. It was dancing on the edge of a razor. Not enough pressure, and Taylor's gangland-style government would continue to destabilize the region to his gain. Too much pressure and the country might collapse into a failed state, ripe for exploitation by criminals and terrorists of every stripe.

Furthermore, Taylor and many of his advisors thought that we were behind the rebels and supporting them covertly with money and arms. We were not, but Taylor believed we were.

That was a danger for the embassy because at some point, if Taylor was losing the war, he might attack the embassy in retribution.

What further complicated our position was that the rebels were thugs, too. We very much wanted to see a new government, and it was obvious the only way Taylor would go was if he was forced out, but we did not want to exchange one set of killers for another. We knew precious little about the rebels, but we did not see any nascent George Washingtons out there. More like new Al Capones.

So, the question was how to use the situation to force Taylor out, without the rebels winning? And how did we do this without a bloodbath fight for Monrovia?

The biggest obstacle we faced in getting Taylor to leave was his fear of being indicted for war crimes by the Special Court in Sierra Leone. Increasingly, his advisors were asking me what assurances I could give that, if he left, we would not indict him.

The difficulty was twofold. First, we did not control the Special Court. Second, I think Taylor did not believe that we did not control the court.

Under no circumstances would Taylor leave the country if he thought he would be arrested and sent to prison in Sierra Leone, as he so richly deserved. He would stay in Liberia and, if he had to, flee into the bush with his core followers and continue the war as best he could, or die trying.

An intricate fan dance followed between Taylor and myself. His intermediaries said they thought he might agree, for the good of the country, to step down at the end of his current term and not to run again for president. However, he could not step down immediately, since he was "constitutionally obligated" to fill out his current term.

Richard Nixon had stepped down, I responded. Presidents can resign.

Richard Nixon, I was told, had committed a crime. Charles Taylor had not. He had to preserve the integrity of the constitution, or it would mean nothing and lead to instability. The rebel/terrorists would achieve their objective, and this would allow terrorists to triumph through violence. Surely I could see that?

I could see, I said, that the rebels were gaining ground, and that something must be done to end the suffering of the Liberian people. That was true, they admitted. And President Taylor had no problem with a U.S.-led peacekeeping force entering his country to end the war.

I think Taylor was serious. His calculation was that our troops would act as a buffer with the effect of keeping him in power. The U.S. could sponsor peace conferences that he could prolong for months or even years. Ambassador Blaney appropriately called these meetings "Peace Jamborees," since they were all hoopla and no substance.

There was the danger that if, as expected, Taylor was indicted by the Special Court in Sierra Leone for war crimes, a U.S. peace force in the country might grab him and pack him off to stand trial.

But Taylor had faith that his status as a sitting president granted him immunity from prosecution. Legally, it is a tricky business to try to arrest a sitting head of state. To violate that immunity puts all heads of state at risk. George Bush, for instance, could have found himself at risk of arrest when traveling abroad if, for example, Iran had indicted him for war crimes in Iraq and Bush was visiting a country with an extradition treaty with Iran. Furthermore, the fact that Jimmy Carter had observed the election in Liberia and certified that Taylor had actually been elected gave him confidence, I think, that we could not arrest him.

In the end, I think he was wrong. Right or wrong legally, I believe we would have found grounds to arrest him if we were in Liberia in force.

In any event, I told Taylor's people I would let Washington know of the offer. Personally, I thought there wasn't a snowball's chance in hell of a major U.S. intervention.

Sure, we had intervened in Europe to stop the killing in Kosovo. And 5,000 U.S. troops could end the mess in Liberia in a matter of days and have the whole operation under U.N. command in a matter of months, giving us an exit strategy, as the British had finally done to end similar fighting in neighboring Sierra Leone.

But these were just Africans, and the Bush Administration was not about to put boots on the ground in Liberia if it could help it.

CHAPTER 25

The fighting continued, Taylor was running short on ammunition and he needed to get serious about his options. I got the word from his office he wanted to see me for a face-to-face parley.

We met at the same outdoor pavilion on the presidential office grounds where I had last seen him with Ambassador Blaney, only this time the ostriches were kept well away.

Taylor's entourage, however, had grown for this occasion, and included his personal advisor, several of his chief ministers, including his minister of defense, and, of great surprise to me, his vice president, the appropriately named Moses Blah.

I say appropriate because, in most every regard, Mr. Blah had a reputation for being as blah as a man can get. There was nothing remarkable about him, from his appearance to his ambition. He looked blah, he dressed blah and he acted blah. That, I suspected, was exactly what Taylor wanted in a man a "heartbeat" away from the presidency of Liberia. Or, one might more accurately say, a short quick stab in the back with a sharp knife away from the presidency. Taylor knew all about backstabbing and he wanted someone without ambition, guile or any inclination for risk-taking in the vice president job. He found such a man in Moses Blah.

Even so, Taylor was, according to what I knew, careful to keep Blah uninformed and out of the loop on all major issues of importance.

That Blah and the others were in attendance said to me that Taylor wanted everyone to know exactly what he had to say to the Americans.

There were to be no rumors, no second-guessing by those who might misinterpret or mistake his intentions and act against him based on false assumptions about his plans.

As the rebels closed in, his top men were looking for a safe place to land, which might include on Taylor's back, ready to turn him over to the rebels to curry favor with the new boss in town.

I greeted the president, we shook hands and I sat.

Well, Charlie, I thought, looking at the old brown briefcase Taylor set down next to himself, and which I was sure was full of money and a gun, it is your move. There is nothing like negotiating with a pistol-packing head of state. Not even George Bush carried a gun into Cabinet meetings, and he was from Texas.

Again, I had to suppress the revulsion I felt at being in the presence of a man who was as nasty as they come. More than that, I had to understand him, even put myself in his skin so I could look for weaknesses and the means to manipulate him.

Taylor was as self-absorbed and long-winded as ever. He went on at great length about his "constitutional" responsibilities, and how they limited his freedom of action. He was the president of Liberia, and it was a heavy burden, but one he was sworn to uphold, and his word was his bond. His only concern, his final responsibility, he assured me, was for the welfare of his people. This, from the man whose most famous campaign slogan was, "He killed my ma, he killed my pa, I'm voting for Taylor," because it advertised that the only way for the war-weary population to end the violence was to let Taylor be president.

It was a wonder he did not choke on his own words, but like all good liars I think he believed his own fantasy about what he had become.

He then went on at some length about his concern for how Liberians would remember him in the future, and his legacy.

And here was my opening.

"There has been too much fighting and too much killing," said Taylor. "A way must be found to end it."

Taylor, in the past, had refused to meet directly with rebel leaders to discuss a peace settlement. As long as he held the upper hand, he saw no need. When pressed previously, he had answered, "Would you meet with Osama bin Laden to discuss peace? Why should I be asked to do what you will not? The rebels are terrorists."

I told Taylor that he was right, and his people were suffering. How could we end it?

"I want to meet with you Americans to discuss peace," he told me. "I will send my top advisors to Washington to meet at the State Department. In face-to-face meetings, we might," he said, "find a way out." But it must, Taylor emphasized, happen soon, because the situation was growing critical.

It was a significant admission by Taylor, and a marked departure from my last meeting when he told Ambassador Blaney that the rebels were insignificant and would be defeated in a matter of days. Obviously, he knew his back was to the wall and he needed a way out.

I doubted the State Department would agree to public meetings in Washington for fear of the intense criticism sure to be leveled at the Administration by human rights groups, but meetings somewhere else, in Europe, for instance, seemed possible to me.

"What would we discuss at these meetings?" I asked.

Taylor looked first at his own men, and then he turned to me. "Everything is on the table," he answered.

Clearly, what he said was intended as much for them as for me.

I answered that I thought he was correct that his legacy as the president of Liberia was at stake. He needed to do what was best for his people. The decisions might be difficult, but if he made the right ones, his place in Liberian history would be assured.

He nodded. He said he understood and agreed. Now was the time to show what kind of man and what kind of leader he was.

He might need to make personal sacrifices for the good of his country, I said. "This is your chance to be remembered as one of the great men of Liberia. The president who, for the good of his people, made the difficult decision to step down so that lives could be saved. I am also concerned for your safety if the rebels take the city. I am concerned for your people and the slaughter that will follow." I felt like gagging, but what I had done was open a door that allowed him to leave and survive, while subtly drawing his attention to his certain fate if he stayed.

He agreed.

I appreciated, I said, that his choices would not be easy.

"I am ready," he said, "to work with you Americans. I am ready to meet to discuss how to bring peace to Liberia, whatever the cost to myself."

I looked at him. "You must step down. Are you prepared to go that far, if that is what is required to bring peace to Liberia?"

As the acting American ambassador, I was not worried about what Taylor's reaction to my statement might be right then, but Taylor had killed men for suggesting less. Taylor could not afford to kill me, at least not then and not there. But the question was not entirely risk-free. "Accidents" could happen later, after all.

This really was dancing with the devil.

Taylor looked significantly at his advisors and then at me.

"Everything," he repeated, solemnly and clearly, "is on the table."

Mine was the beginning of the effort to force Taylor out, but only the beginning. When Taylor finally did go into exile in Nigeria, he had vacillated back and forth for several weeks, due largely to his fear of indictment by the Special Court and how far the rebels were succeeding or failing in capturing Monrovia. Many after me continued to push him, including several African heads of state, but most especially Ambassador Blaney after his return to Liberia. In the end, as the rebels were closing in, it was Ambassador Blaney who succeeded in coaxing Taylor out, with some behind-the-scenes help from other sources I cannot reveal, but this meeting with Taylor was the first move to end the war..

CHAPTER 26

I reported to Washington the details of my conversation. I thought, I said, we had an opportunity. Taylor was clearly looking for an escape in case the rebels succeeded. He did not want a repeat of President Doe's fate.

I emphasized the importance, as I saw it, of massaging his ego. His desire not to be castrated, and his need to feel that his personal "sacrifice" in stepping down would make him a hero, could act as a push-pull that would get him out the door. Much as I might personally despise Taylor, and as much as he richly deserved to be castrated, my first concern was to stop the fighting and save as many Liberians as we could.

The fly in the ointment was the Special Court in Sierra Leone. If they indicted Taylor, he would resist leaving Liberia unless he was given immunity from prosecution, and without it he would stay and go down fighting. Monrovia would become a wasteland and the country would almost certainly descend into the complete lawlessness of a failed state. It was already on the precipice.

As expected, a meeting between Taylor and State Department officials in Washington was ruled out. However, an American delegation, including Ambassador Blaney, was assigned to meet with Taylor's representatives in Europe.

I believe Taylor was probably ready to deal at that moment if given immunity from the Special Court. The problem was, as often as we explained that the Special Court was independent and not under our jurisdiction, Taylor and many of his advisors refused to believe it.

Attempts were made to sound out the court on their willingness to forego indicting Taylor for the sake of ending the war in Liberia and saving lives, and they were having none of it. They would make no promises or commitments. Justice, they said, would have to run its course.

I am a supporter of justice, although there is often a difference between the law and justice. My problem was that I cared more about preventing mass slaughter and chaos than about seeing Charles Taylor behind bars. I wanted both, but the reality seemed to be that we could have one or the other.

I was on a collision course with the court. It nearly got me killed.

CHAPTER 27

The Special Court in Sierra Leone was established by the United Nations with international support for the laudable goal of bringing to trial those responsible for war crimes during the horrific civil war in that country.

An independent special court, supported by funds and staff from the international community, was established because the criminal justice system in Sierra Leone was so weakened and dysfunctional that it lacked the institutional capacity to properly carry out the mission of holding people responsible for war crimes. Furthermore, it was recognized that there were many people outside of Sierra Leone who had a hand in promoting the war who would be beyond the reach of Sierra Leonean courts, but not beyond the reach of an international special court.

Finally, although established by the U.N., the court was independent of the U.N., answering to no government or international body anywhere, which was highly unusual. While this did make it independent, it also removed all the checks and balances that normally apply to courts. The only check on the operation of the court was financial, in that those financing its operations could withdraw their support and the court would cease to be able to operate.

The result was that the pursuit of "justice" became the obsession of the court to the complete exclusion of every other consideration. For the man who came to run the court, no force on earth could deter him from his single-minded path, no matter the cost to anyone else.

It was too much power concentrated in the hands of one man.

In the court's defense, their rationale was that those responsible for war crimes had to be held accountable to stop the cycle of violence in Africa, and to set an example that where powerful men and women commit atrocities, they will be, and can be, punished. Future thugs need to know that there is no escape from the consequences of their crimes.

If those who committed atrocities were allowed to negotiate deals to escape justice, it would act as an incentive for brutal men to follow brutal paths to power, knowing that if they failed they could always work a deal. Jailing dictators would deter future violence, and although in the short term innocents might suffer, in the long term more would be saved.

It does not work that way. Most people do not commit atrocities knowing it is wrong. In societies that do have strong institutions to enforce the rule of law, some actually do refrain from committing crimes for fear of the consequences. People like Mosquito, Charles Taylor, Stalin and Adolph Hitler, however, do what they do not because they believe they can wiggle out of paying a price if their plans fail; they do it because they are self-absorbed, opportunistic psychopaths who are fixated on achieving their ends no matter the cost to others. They do not believe, cannot even conceive, they will fail.

It became clear early on that the Special Court would not work a deal to allow Charles Taylor to escape Liberia. What I did not anticipate was how far they would go to actually work *against* the peace process.

Taylor's representatives did meet with State Department staff, including Ambassador Blaney, in Brussels. Taylor's top people were surprised at the American hard line that Taylor must go, but it did help them to better understand that they needed to also work to coax Taylor to leave. They wanted to survive the war, and understood that as long as Taylor remained, the war would never end. Still, the main sticking point for Taylor was avoiding an indictment by the Special Court, and he was close to leaving if he could get the immunity deal. In exchange, we would get what we wanted (Taylor gone), the fighting would end, and Liberia could try to get back to normal. Our inability to grant immunity, as Taylor saw it, was a refusal on our part to cooperate. What I think Taylor never believed was that immunity was not ours to give.

This seeming refusal to grant Taylor immunity also reinforced the view with some in Taylor's circle that we were, in fact, behind the rebels and supporting them.

We did our best to finesse the issue, pointing out that Taylor had not actually been indicted, but that was about to change.

CHAPTER 28

The consular section of the embassy continued to do its best to create a comprehensive list of Americans still in Liberia and how to contact them in case of an evacuation.

I decided to hold a town hall meeting at the embassy for all those holding an American passport to urge them to leave. The problem was, like the youth group I had already met, many of the Americans were with faith-based charitable programs. They were doing the Lord's work, and most would not leave because the Lord was with them.

I, on the other hand, have always lived by the maxim that God helps those who help themselves. And I knew that if fighting broke out in the capital, and some of them became trapped in desperate situations, my people would have to risk their lives to try and save them.

Of course, I was one to talk. What the hell was I still doing in Monrovia? I was there because I took an oath to work for the American people, and I was staying because it was my job and I had promised John Blaney that I would not close his embassy. I was sure that, as far as the Lord was concerned, I was on my own.

So in reality there was very little difference between us, except they worked for God and I worked for the American people.

We put the word out about the meeting and made arrangements to host everyone in a large dining hall on the embassy compound where the staff generally had lunch. About a hundred and fifty people came. I was counting on them to network with additional Americans they knew, who would talk to other Americans, and the multiplier effect would reach most everyone who needed to hear the message. In a place like Liberia, that was how communications worked.

I always admired the style of Abraham Lincoln, who often conveyed a message through a story, so I opened with a story about a man caught in a terrible flood. When the water was up to his door, a man with a rowboat came by the house and offered to take him to safety. He refused, exclaiming, "I believe in the Lord and the Lord will protect me!"

This got the attention of the people in the room.

The water continued to rise, I said, and soon it was at the top floor of his home. Another man in a rowboat came and offered to take him to safety. Again he refused and exclaimed, "I believe in the Lord and the Lord will protect me!"

The water kept rising and the man found himself on the roof of his home with a raging torrent of water rushing past. A helicopter spotted him and lowered a rope to take him to safety. The man refused, exclaiming, "I believe in the Lord and the Lord will protect me!"

The helicopter left, the water washed the house away and the man drowned. At the gates of heaven, he was met by the Lord and he cried, "Oh, Lord, I had faith in you and yet you let me drown! Why, Lord?"

And the Lord answered, "For God's sake, I sent you two rowboats and a helicopter. What more did you want?"

I looked at the audience and said, "The river is rising, folks, and the rowboat is here that can take you out. You need to get in that boat."

I then gave a detailed report on what we knew about the rebel advances on the capital, pointing out that the international airport could close very suddenly, and urged them to leave before they were trapped.

Many protested that they had important work to do and people depended upon them.

I said I understood, but it was my duty to let them know they were at risk if they stayed, and that I might not have the resources to help if they became isolated in any future fighting. I sympathized with their commitment to their missions, but said that if they had to stay, that did not mean that any dependents with them should stay, and they should send out their spouses and children. It was one thing to put yourself at risk for what you believed in, but it was quite another to put your family at risk.

Most of them listened to that, but sad to say, not all of them. I will never understand why some people keep their children in harm's way when they have the option to keep them safe.

CHAPTER 29

The Economic Community of West African States, known as ECOWAS, included almost all the nations of West Africa, among them such regional powerhouses as Nigeria and Senegal. Several ECOWAS member states had become active in trying to resolve the civil war in Liberia, both because they wanted to do what they could to end the fighting, but also because it was destabilizing the region. A collapsed Liberian state threatened them. Already, Liberian refugees were flooding into all the neighboring states, countries that could ill afford to take care of them. They also had a reputation for creating problems wherever they went, as many former fighters, brutal men whose only training was in the art of banditry and war, were often among those fleeing.

The head ECOWAS negotiator was a Nigerian general who came to Liberia on a fact-finding mission and to speak to Taylor. What was left of the foreign missions in Liberia also met with him, myself included.

It was agreed that pressure should be brought to bear on Taylor to attend a peace conference with the rebels. Such a conference could not take place in Liberia because the rebel leaders would not risk coming to Monrovia, fearing, with justification, that Taylor would use the opportunity to kill them, and Taylor would not go to areas of the country controlled by them because he feared, with justification, that they would kill him.

Neighboring Ghana offered to host the conference, and a reluctant Taylor finally agreed to attend. A great deal of arm-twisting was also done with the rebels to get them to go. The conference finally took place in early June.

When Taylor left, he took almost his entire senior Cabinet with him, essentially leaving behind only Moses Blah, his vice president. Taylor did this because it made him nervous to be out of the country and he did not want to leave anyone behind who might get ambitious and try to take over in his absence. Still, he had to leave someone behind, and Moses got the job. It was to nearly cost him his life, and that was indirectly my fault.

We had hopes for the peace conference. Indications were that Taylor was at least willing to consider leaving Liberia, although he would do all he could to stay if he saw a way to do it and live. But the military pressure continued to build and his options were closing.

A deal for an interim government was in the works. A peacekeeping force composed of ECOWAS member state troops to be largely funded by the United States and Europe would support it. The peacekeepers would be charged with the mission of disarming all the combatants, both rebels and government. Furthermore, since they would essentially be in charge of internal security, the rebels could lay down their arms and join the political process without fear of Taylor's forces assassinating them at the first opportunity.

I cannot take credit for this plan. Ambassador John Blaney was the man behind it. Although I was still running his embassy, by this time John was very active behind the scenes outside of Liberia doing all he could to finalize a settlement along the lines I have outlined.

Then the Special Court struck.

They had already infuriated me just before this by directly contacting a Liberian employee of the embassy to request that he help smuggle a prosecution witness against Taylor out of Liberia and into Sierra Leone. The employee was responsible for helping to clear embassy staff and shipments through the airport. His contacts at the airport were excellent, and because of his status as a representative of the American embassy he could get the attention of the highest-level government security people at the airport.

The staff at the Special Court had been repeatedly warned to contact the ambassador of any American embassy before requesting assistance from a staff member. The State Department had set this requirement upon them because in the past they had tried to work around ambassadors in getting our embassies to perform errands for them. In short, they knew perfectly well that in asking this employee to help them, they were breaking their agreement. However, whomever it was they wanted to get to Sierra Leone, they wanted him bad.

What they were doing was particularly egregious, and indicative of the cavalier attitude they held about putting other people's lives at risk. In this instance, if my Liberian employee had done what they requested and helped this individual board a plane out of Liberia, Taylor would have learned about it and ordered the man killed. It really upsets me when someone puts the life of another at risk, especially when that man is someone whose safety is my responsibility.

Second, had this happened it would have confirmed to Taylor that, despite our protestations, the American government was working hand-in-glove with the Special Court. Word would have spread, and every employee at the embassy, Liberian and American, would have been at increased risk of attack from Taylor's undisciplined militias. Tensions were already running high.

Fortunately, the employee had the good sense to speak to my Security Chief about the contact, and we let him know he was never to take on any job assigned to him by the Special Court unless specifically authorized to do so by Ambassador Blaney or me.

What I found particularly offensive in the whole affair was that when I complained to Washington about the incident, the Court at first denied they had done it, and then they said they had the permission of my Security Chief to contact the man. It was a lie.

Apparently, the pursuit of justice not only allows you to put other people at risk, but you get to lie, as well, in the name of a higher cause.

What the Court did next was even worse.

When Taylor left Liberia to attend the peace conference, no sooner did he get to Ghana than the Court publicly indicted him and called for his arrest as a war criminal. They called the president of Ghana to demand that Taylor be held in detention until they could arrange for him to be transported to Sierra Leone for trial.

It was a stupid thing to do for multiple reasons.

First, anyone who knew Africa could have told the Court that Ghana would never, ever arrest Taylor and send him to Sierra Leone. Africa is littered with political leaders who, from time to time, find it necessary to flee coups in their countries. They know that if a precedent is set for returning former leaders to stand trial or, more likely, face outright execution, that very thing might well happen to them later. It is accepted etiquette not to arrest present or former African heads of state.

So the Court was wasting its time.

Second, this killed the chances for a peace agreement. Now that Taylor was indicted, he had to get back to Liberia (which he quickly did, courtesy of a plane supplied to him by the government of Ghana), and he now had no incentive to make peace, but rather had his back to the wall and every incentive to fight to the last man, woman and child in Liberia. If he was going down, he was going to take everyone with him. The Court had set the scene for a Rwandan-scale massacre in Liberia.

Incredibly, on top of that, the Court issued a press release asserting that as an indicted war criminal, Taylor should no longer be recognized as the head of state of Liberia and that no one was to negotiate a peace treaty with him.

It was idiocy to suggest that there was an alternative to negotiating with Taylor. Who were we going to talk to? Taylor controlled the army. Like it or not, Taylor was the government. If Taylor did not agree to a peace accord, there would not be one. It was as if the Court was saying, "Don't talk to the man with the gun pointed at your head. He's not the legitimate owner of the gun, so he doesn't have the right to pull the trigger."

Right.

CHAPTER 30

When the indictment was announced on the international news services, Taylor's militia forces went on a rampage. Jeeps full of heavily armed men drove past the embassy, waving guns at us.

Fearing that Taylor really might not come back, many soldiers decided it was time to steal whatever they could while they still had the ability to steal it.

Pro- and anti-Taylor riots broke out.

Reports poured in that Americans were blamed for the indictment, and that Taylor's troops were looking for Americans on the street to punish.

Liberian employees of the embassy were also at risk.

Something had to be done to calm the situation. I decided to call the most senior member of the government in the country: Moses Blah.

I told him we were concerned about the situation in Monrovia. I said that troops brandishing guns were driving by the embassy and Americans were being threatened. I reminded him of his government's responsibility to control the military, and that if my embassy was attacked there would be heavy consequences. He needed to act to stop the militias from harming Americans. I repeated that we were not behind the indictment, and that I still had hopes a peace agreement could end the war in Liberia.

Moses said he understood and would do all he could to control the army.

Next, we called one of the senior commanders in Taylor's military, one we knew had influence with the unpredictable and undisciplined militia forces. I repeated to him the message that the situation must not get out of hand. If there was an attack, or if Americans were killed, there would be consequences.

What those consequences would be, I was not sure, since I was not convinced our government would do much more than order all of us out of the country, but I made the threat sound as ominous as possible. My hope was that they thought American troops were on the way and people would be arrested.

Again, high-stakes poker.

About a half an hour later, the general was on the radio. He said that President Taylor had not been arrested and was returning to Liberia. He ordered all troops to stand down. Looting would not be tolerated. Punishments for those who broke the law would be swift and severe.

The streets quieted, the looting stopped and the harassment of American citizens ceased.

Well, I thought, nothing like a good day's work.

Then Taylor got back.

CHAPTER 31

What I had not counted on was Taylor's larger-than-life paranoia. He was absolutely convinced we orchestrated the peace conference as a trap. Phase one was to get the Special Court to issue the indictment as soon as he left the country. Phase two, he was sure, was to work with collaborators in Liberia to put in place a puppet regime to replace him, one that would do our bidding.

He immediately set out to uncover the moles in his government. He hauled in the general who had been on the radio and questioned him. Why had he been on the radio? Who authorized him to speak for the government? Charles Taylor was the president, not him. How dare he? How much had the Americans paid him?

The general realized his life was on the line, sure that Taylor was convinced he had been part of a conspiracy against him. If he denied there was an American plot, it would make it look like he was that much deeper in it and Taylor would kill him.

Yes, he said, the Americans had plotted against him, but he was not the real conspirator. He had simply played along so that he could learn who really was behind the whole affair. Best of all, he said, he succeeded. He knew who the American puppet was.

"Who?" Taylor demanded.

"Moses Blah. Check his cell phone. You'll see that he has been talking to the Americans."

Taylor hauled Moses in from his home in the middle of the night.

"I know what you have done," Taylor told him.

Moses did not understand. What had he done?

"You conspired with the Americans to take my place. The general has confirmed it to me. How much did they offer you to stab me in the back?"

Moses was dumbfounded. He denied any plot.

"I have proof," said Taylor. He showed Blah his own cell phone; the record of past calls clearly documented that he spoke to the American embassy.

"Is it a crime for the American embassy to call me?" he protested. He told Taylor what I said.

Taylor did not believe him. In Taylor's universe, the conspiracy made perfect sense. It was, ironically, what Taylor himself would have done in Moses's place. He arrested Moses. He contemplated having him executed on the spot.

There were people who did call me during the crisis who indicated a desire to work with us to bring down Taylor. But I did not call them, they called us, and poor Moses was not one of them. Paranoids like Taylor often destroy themselves by killing those closest to them, and Taylor nearly did that with Moses.

I am glad he did not. I cannot say that I exactly liked Moses. He was a stooge of Taylor's, after all. But he was a fairly innocuous stooge, as stooges go, a guy just trying to survive in an ocean of sharks, and I did not want his blood on my conscience.

Ironically, Ambassador John Blaney would later convince Taylor in a meeting that we were not behind the indictment, or behind any plot to oust him, by saying, "Mr. President, if we had wanted you dead, you would be dead."

In Taylor's paranoid universe, where the United States is all-powerful, that made sense to him. My hat is off to John, however, because I never would have thought of telling him that. Not long after John said it, Taylor released Moses from detention and reinstated him as vice president.

CHAPTER 32

Shortly after the arrest of Moses, Taylor went on the radio to address the nation.

There had been a foreign plot to oust him, he proclaimed. Sadly, he said, there were Liberians who were complicit in that plot. The vice president had been one of them, and he was now under arrest. He had been offered three million dollars to cooperate by the Western embassy behind the plot.

How Taylor came to the figure of three million dollars, I am not sure. Perhaps the general Taylor first talked to had said that I offered them three million dollars to implicate Blah as a stooge in our effort to overthrow Taylor. If I'd had three million dollars to pay, I probably could have convinced one of Taylor's men to kill him.

Taylor never named the American embassy, but we were the only Western embassy in town. He went on to excoriate us in his address, again without specifically naming me, but making it clear whom he was referring to. Not only had this Western power tried to stab him in the back, but we were behind the rebels, as well, which was why he was having such trouble suppressing them. The Liberian people were suffering, and this embassy was to blame.

This was dangerous brinkmanship. As it was, we had the occasional truckload of Taylor's heavily armed men driving by the embassy. They were often drunk and/or high on drugs. God only knew what they might do, especially now that Taylor was directly and publicly blaming us for supporting the rebels.

In addition, despite my best efforts to get Americans to leave, there were still several hundred in the country and they could also become the targets of Taylor's men looking to pay us back for our supposed support of the rebels.

I made phone calls to people we knew in the government, condemning the accusations. I made an appointment with the Ministry of Foreign Affairs, where I threatened to close the embassy if these false charges were not publicly withdrawn. Ironically, even Taylor did not want us to actually close the embassy. If the rebels succeeded in coming after him, he might still need us to help negotiate his way out of the mess he would be in. Not that we would help him if we did not have to, but Ambassador Blaney and I had made it amply clear that our first priority was to save lives, and that was something Taylor might use to escape if he was trapped.

The ministry officials said they understood. They clearly were worried by my threat. They would talk to Taylor right away. I said I could not wait long. The president had recklessly put my embassy and Americans living in Liberia in danger. I was responsible, and I would close if I thought it was my only option to protect my people.

It was a hollow threat. I had promised John to keep his embassy open until he got back, and that was what I intended to do, but Taylor did not know that. Again, high-stakes poker.

I arrived at the Ministry in a heavily armored sport utility vehicle supplied to the embassy by the State Department. Since I was on official business, we prominently flew the U.S. stars and stripes and the flag that indicated that the acting ambassador was in the vehicle. The flags were mounted on short poles on the front of the vehicle. Everyone in Monrovia knew the car and what it meant when those flags were displayed.

We came to a checkpoint manned by two guards, one old and the other young. They did not wave us through, as usual, but forced us to stop.

The old guy, clutching his AK-47, glared at us, his eyes bloodshot and sullen. The good news was that the armor on the car would stop AK-47 ammunition; for a while, anyway.

The other, younger soldier had a rocket-propelled grenade, or RPG. It is a tube about four feet long that fires a rocket with a sizable explosive charge. The charge is mounted on the front of the tube, large and roughly oval in shape.

The soldier stared at our car with dark, glazed and hate-filled eyes. There was no doubt how he felt. He brought the RPG to his shoulder and aimed it at our front windshield, his finger curled around the trigger.

A direct hit from an RPG would reduce the car to a smoking ruin. We crept slowly through the checkpoint.

The soldier kept the RPG trained on us. I kept looking straight at him, and he stared right back. I could see the wheels turning in his head. To fire, or not to fire?

We were too close to shoot. The explosion would kill us all, him included, but he kept staring down the sights at me, his finger still on the trigger.

Then we were past him and starting down a hill. This was the most dangerous moment, because now the son of a bitch could launch the RPG without killing himself. I did not look back. The seconds ticked away, and then we cleared another hill and were out of their line of sight.

It was a close call. Exactly what I had warned the Ministry might happen—that one of Taylor's armed rabble might decide to take a shot at us—had nearly come to pass.

When I got back to the embassy, I called our contacts in the government and informed them of the incident, excoriating them for putting the embassy at risk. I reported back to Washington, and representatives of the State Department called in Liberia's ambassador to read him the riot act.

Taylor did tone down his rhetoric against us after that.

CHAPTER 33

The situation got hotter. The indictment of Taylor by the Special Court encouraged the rebel leaders to push harder on the military front. They smelled Taylor's blood in the water, and they did not want a peace agreement if they could win an outright military victory and assume power without any restraints imposed by negotiating a political process for change. Once again, the effect of the Special Court's action was to spur on the killing.

One of the offices in the embassy was that of the Defense Attaché. One of my most valuable staff members was an army sergeant we called Fergie. He was supposed to be a kind of secretary in that office, but in fact he was one of the best-connected people in the embassy. He was a true eccentric as only the military can produce them: a beer-drinking, high-school-educated, no-nonsense, straight-talking, fearless and risk-taking U.S. soldier that you see in all the war movies, only he was the real McCoy. My main worry was that he was going to get himself killed. He was forever driving to places where he should not have gone to gather intelligence, no matter how many times I ordered him not to take unnecessary risks.

He was just back from a trip north of Monrovia, and what he reported worried me.

Large numbers of people were on the move. Refugee camps to the north of us were emptying, and a sea of humanity was headed for Monrovia.

These were people who knew what fighting was, and when it was time to get out of harm's way. Even more, in the refugee camps there were at least minimal services available, including food and water. Leaving the camps meant abandoning that lifeline for a new location where God only knew what support might be obtainable. It was no small risk for them to take, but they were taking it. Something was up and it had to be serious.

I called my senior staff together to review the latest information. I then asked each person what he or she thought we should do. At the top of my list of things to consider was whether or not to request a drawdown of the embassy to a skeleton staff level and an evacuation of all Americans we did not absolutely need at post.

About two thirds said we should sit tight and make no changes. We had been here before, and there would be time to draw down later if it came to that. That was Fergie's opinion. The trouble was, Fergie wasn't afraid of anything. I was. I had to be.

About a third of the staff thought we should draw down. The signs were ominous, and it was time to reduce our numbers to the minimum. Not that we had a lot of people as it was. If I recall, my entire American staff, including six Marine guards, numbered about thirty-five.

An embassy is not a democracy, and the final decision rested with me, but I wanted everyone to feel their opinion had been taken into account.

I decided it was time to draw down.

We took a hard look at our staff to decide whom we could do without. I got the number down to twenty-three and told the rest to pack their bags. They should not expect to be back, I said, any time soon. I called Washington on a secure line and discussed the request to draw down. Washington concurred, the orders were issued and those selected left.

Two days later the fighting came to Monrovia.

CHAPTER 34

I wasn't worried when it began. Monrovia is situated on a number of islands connected by bridges. To the north of the embassy was Bushrod Island, the location of the main port facilities. The only way the rebels could reach Bushrod Island from the north was across a long narrow bridge.

It looked to me like a perfect chokepoint, militarily. All Taylor needed was to station his troops on the northern tip of Bushrod Island and keep the rebels from crossing the bridge. If worse came to worse, Taylor could always blow the bridge, although that would make retaking the area to the north difficult for government forces later.

So I expected the fighting would stay north of Bushrod. We did, however, begin to hear the distant thunder of heavy mortar fire.

As the day wore on, the battle came closer, until in the late afternoon I heard the crackle of small arms fire. The mortars sounded like nearby thunder.

A viably shaken political officer on my staff came to my office. Friends of his in the government had called him. The rebels, they said, were across the bridge. The fighting was on Bushrod Island itself.

"If they couldn't stop them at the bridge, what will stop them now?" I asked.

He shook his head. "Nothing. I expect the rebels will overrun Monrovia tonight."

I ordered in all the staff. I wanted the embassy buttoned down and no one was to be out roaming the streets. We had enough food, water, and fuel oil to last us a week. I told everyone to use as little water and electricity as possible so we could stretch our resources to the max. No one was to flush a toilet if it was just pee.

I got on the phone to Washington to let the State Department know. By this time, the Department had a twenty-four-hour task force to monitor our situation and lend whatever support they could. Mostly, I emphasized the need to contact the rebel leadership and tell them to avoid firing on the embassy compound. If they succeeded in ousting Taylor, they would want U.S. recognition of their new government and they would want assistance. They were not going to get either if any of their forces attacked us.

To tell the truth, I was not afraid of the rebels. It was Taylor's men who had me biting my nails. I could hold off quite a few of them with the Marines I had, as ill-disciplined as Taylor's men were. But a concerted attack would overwhelm us, and if they started lobbing mortars into the compound, people would die. What I really needed was additional U.S. troops.

I requested that Washington send in a team of Navy SEALs to beef up my perimeter defenses, the more the better.

American citizens were now clamoring for evacuation. Although the government still controlled the airport, which was some distance from the fighting, the major international airlines were no longer landing there. Their insurance companies had declared they would not cover planes landing at Robert's Field, and no international carrier would risk landing a plane without insurance coverage. A few planes were still coming in from neighboring African countries, but the scene at the airport was a madhouse. People with reservations were losing their seats to passengers willing to pay ticketing agents big bribes.

I needed enough helicopters to get at least 100 people out, probably more. I did not have them.

CHAPTER 35

I got no sleep that night. The next day dawned, and to my surprise we found the rebels still on Bushrod Island to the north. Monrovia had not been overrun, although the fighting still sounded intense. Occasional stray rounds of automatic rifle fire landed in the compound and hissed overhead through the branches of the trees.

I was puzzled. How could the rebels cross the bridge to Bushrod Island and yet not take the city? What we did not know was that the rebels were really hardly more than an expeditionary force of about 200 men. Their intent was to push on Taylor's forces to search for weaknesses that could be exploited later by the main rebel army. They were as surprised as anyone to find themselves in the port. It was a testament to how weak Taylor's forces were, and how low their morale and will to fight were, that this small rebel force had crossed the bridge. They simply did not have enough men to take the whole city.

There was some good news. Washington was supporting my request for additional military personnel to secure the embassy. The trouble was, the men were available but transportation to get them to the embassy was not. Twenty SEALs were headed to Freetown, in neighboring Sierra Leone, but they would be stuck there until helicopters could be found to bring them directly into the embassy compound. It might be days or even weeks before U.S. military choppers would be in position.

As I knew from my previous assignment as Charge d'Affairs in Freetown, we had two helicopters under contract to our embassy there, big Russian MI-8s that could hold up to twenty people each. However, they were not U.S. military, but belonged to an American firm who flew them under contract to the State Department, as I stated earlier. And, just like the international airlines that would no longer fly into Monrovia because no insurance carrier would cover them, this American firm was reluctant to let its choppers go into Monrovia with a battle raging.

The good news was that this company was used to taking some risks. They had operated in Sierra Leone through most of the war years. With some arm-twisting, we eventually convinced them to make the trip. A day later, the SEALs arrived.

SEALs are as impressive a set of trained killers as you will find anywhere, and I was ecstatic to have them. I have seldom felt as much relief in my life as when I saw those two great big blue helicopters emerge out of the mist over the ocean, land at our helipad and deliver those men. They jumped out and took up defensive positions, rifles at the ready, as the choppers unloaded one at a time.

Their commanders came to my office where we briefed them on the situation, studied the layout of the embassy, and I let them get to work stationing their men strategically around our perimeter. They were lean, efficient, well equipped (including night-vision gear) and no-nonsense. It was going to be a lot easier to sleep at night.

What I did not know at the time was that the Pentagon sent the SEALs in with the mission to evacuate and close the embassy. The SEALs never told me this, in retrospect I think because in the briefing I made it clear that we were staying, and only a direct order from Ambassador Blaney or President Bush would persuade me to close. I think at that point they decided to wait for Ambassador Blaney to return so they could confront him.

CHAPTER 36

Just before the fighting started, refugees appeared outside our embassy gates. At first, it was a few individuals, a man or a woman carrying personal items on their backs. Then a few more. Then more. Soon, it was a steady stream, and then a river of humanity, all headed for our gates, until the street in front of the embassy was practically impassable.

They came because we were the United States government in Liberia. They came looking for help and protection. They came because they had no place else to go. The Americans, they thought, will not let us down.

There was nothing I could do for them. At the height of the crisis, there were somewhere in the vicinity of 10,000 people in front of the embassy. I did not have a fraction of what was needed to help feed, clothe or care of them.

They had walked for days. They were tired, hungry and thirsty. They wanted to know why we wouldn't help them.

We forced them back from the gates and set razor wire around the entrances.

Mothers held up infants. If you won't take us, they shouted, at least take our children. Save my child. Please take my child. Don't let my children die.

And there was nothing I could do. I had no facilities to house children, no one to look after them and no medicine to treat them.

It broke my heart. I wanted to do more than sit there behind my barricade. I wanted to help those poor, abused people, the victims of evil men who should have cared about their own people more than their own blind ambition to become the next thug in charge of this poor benighted country, but there was nothing I could do. I was trying to bring peace to their country, a peace that would end their misery and allow them to lead lives approaching something normal, without the constant fear of murder by their own armed forces or those of the rebels, and that was the best I could offer. We were in touch with aid groups to see what support we might be able to get from them, but with fighting in the port nothing was coming into the country.

It got worse.

The day after the SEALs arrived, the commander and I inspected the placement of his troops. At one location on our compound wall that looked out over the sea of refugee faces, the commander said, "Sir, I need your authorization for something."

"Yes?" I said.

"Yes, sir. If those people out there get desperate, and they start scaling the walls to come in here, I need your permission to open fire. We will try not to kill them, but if they are determined to come in, we will have to shoot to kill. Do I have your orders to proceed, sir?"

I looked at the sea of faces looking up at me from the street below, the faces of men, women and children who, but for the grace of God, I could just as easily be one of, along with my own family. I looked at the faces of innocent people who had come here because they thought so much of America that they believed that we would, that we could, never abandon them. I looked at the faces of people who just wanted a break, needed someone to reach out a helping hand and keep them going one more day, or hour, or minute. They wanted to live, and they needed a friend, so they had come to us, to America.

"Sir?" said the commander. "If they come into this compound, we lose control. They will cover every patch of ground until there is standing room only. We won't be able to land helicopters, meaning we won't be able to get ourselves out if we need to."

"And," I said, "the water and food I have on hand would not last them a day. I know. I know."

"Do I have your agreement?"

It was the hardest thing I have ever had to do in my life. There is hardly a day I do not think about the next words out of my mouth.

"Yes," I said, "try to avoid it at all costs, but shoot if they start coming over the walls. I order it."

It never came to that. They never got so desperate or angry that they tried to force their way in while I was there. Thank God, because I doubt I could have lived with myself had innocent people died on my order.

I had promised John Blaney I would keep his embassy open until he got back. I never dreamed just how much he was asking of me. I know, intellectually, that keeping the embassy open was, in the end, instrumental in ending the war. If the embassy had closed, tens of thousands of people would have died in the fighting and chaos that followed. Liberia might well have become a failed state, a haven for all the ugliest kinds of criminals, terrorists and opportunists that crawl out from under the rocks of this world when the chance presents itself, just as Charles Taylor had done. But that would never have erased from my mind the faces of the people looking up at me just then, the people who had come to me looking for an act of humanity.

Green Lantern would never have agreed to such a thing. I had to. I suppose there, at that instant, the child in me fled, never to return.

CHAPTER 37

Taylor rallied his troops. He went to the front with his senior military commanders, inspiring and cajoling his men into action. It worked. In the heavy fight that followed, he pushed the rebels out of Bushrod Island and back across the bridge to the north.

I was surprised because we did not yet know how small the rebel force really was. On the other hand, we did know that once they refitted and reinforced, they would be back.

I still needed to find a way to evacuate Americans, and I did not have one.

Then I received good news. The French representatives in Monrovia told us that French military forces in neighboring Ivory Coast were coming to pull out European Community citizens, and they were willing to take Americans. They were sending a troop transport ship with helicopters, and they had the space to hold several hundred evacuees.

We swung into high gear. My staff was greatly reduced, which meant those remaining were working 24/7. I was routinely getting phone calls from Washington during the night, and I was seldom getting more than two or three hours of sleep.

We had to get word out to the American community that we could pull them out.

We had to get people registered to determine that they were actually Americans.

There were many children born in the U.S. whose parents were Liberians. Only one parent or guardian was allowed to accompany them.

That was not my rule because I would have allowed both parents to go, but that was not my call to make.

We had to let people know they were allowed only ten pounds of baggage.

We had to make arrangements for people to stay overnight on the embassy compound despite the limited accommodations, food and water. We were, in the end, to get about 150 people out, and we only had thirty-six hours to get it done.

We had crowds in front of the embassy all claiming to be Americans and asking to be evacuated. Our first task was to sort them out.

Then, of course, we had to coordinate with the French.

The local French representatives were terrific. I often found it true of the French that the lower down you went in their bureaucracy, the more friendly and reasonable the people were. The higher you went, well, the more they assumed the demeanor one expects of the French.

The French wanted to use my helipad as the location from which to move everyone. To do that, we had to organize a system for moving E.U. citizens into our compound. The E.U. compound was next door to our embassy, and it was suggested we knock a hole in our wall to let the people through. My security officer was adamantly opposed to this because the E.U. compound would be essentially empty during the evacuation and might quickly fill up with Liberian refugees who could use the break to enter our area, resulting in them getting shot.

The wisdom of this was later proven when, after I left, crowds of Liberians did try to break into the compound. They were held off with tear gas and no one was injured, but it was a close call.

Instead, we organized a shuttle system to move everyone. That was fine with the local E.U. reps, but it was not fine with the French general leading the French military units conducting the evacuation.

He did not like the idea of using our helipad at all, since he felt it made the operation look like a joint U.S.-French program. He wanted to rub it in our faces that the French were rescuing helpless Americans because the U.S.G. could not.

The problem was that the E.U. compound had no helipad. So the general insisted one be jury-rigged, which was done on a stony and uneven rock outcropping overlooking the sea.

It was clearly a dangerous place to land a chopper, especially considering they were picking up civilians of varying ages. From where I stood watching it happen, it looked like the rotating chopper blades (the helicopters kept their engines running for quick departure in case of mortar attack) were within a foot or two of the people crossing the landing pad to climb aboard. This clearly put people at risk, but French "dominance" over the U.S. in Africa was clearly asserted.

When the French finished taking out the E.U. citizens, they came to our compound. The first chopper that landed disgorged several French commandos in combat fatigues who secured the already-secure helipad and hunkered down, staring fiercely at everyone. We began loading our people, and as we settled down into a routine of ferrying everyone out to the transport ship, all of us, including our French military guests, relaxed.

All of the American embassy staff deserve special recognition for service above and beyond the call of duty, but special mention has to be given to Dante Paradiso, a junior officer at the embassy.

When I was forced to draw down staff, by all rights Dante had no business staying. As a junior officer, he was the youngest and least experienced member of my staff. The trouble was, he was also very, very good, and I needed to keep the people I knew I could rely on when the action got hot. Dante was such a person, and I sent out more senior people while I kept him.

During the evacuation, the prudence of this choice was readily apparent. Dante worked two days straight without any break or sleep, organizing the details of the operation and processing the Americans who went. In many cases, it was like herding cats. He did it, and I am certain I could not have accomplished the evacuation successfully without him. Before joining the Foreign Service, Dante had been a lawyer making twice what he made as a Foreign Service officer. He joined because of his commitment to public service. He more than demonstrated his commitment that day. He has since published a book about this period in Liberia: *The Embassy: A Story of War and Diplomacy*. It's a terrific read.

As I passed along the line of the evacuees, overseeing the operation, I noticed the adult members of the college group I had spoken to a couple of weeks earlier when I advised them to leave. These were the ones who told me, with some hostility, that they were in Liberia to do

God's work, and He would protect them. They avoided making eye contact with me. Naturally, they did not thank us for hauling them out of harm's way. I did not expect it.

Most of the students, however, did come shake my hand, warmly expressing their gratitude for our help.

CHAPTER 38

was getting calls from Washington asking me if it was time to close the embassy. What could we accomplish by staying?

They told me I was putting people at risk. Was it worth a life, or more, to keep the flag flying in such a Godforsaken place?

What were our national interests?

I answered that lives were on the line. We had to do what we could to stop the fighting, and we could do little if we lost our presence in Monrovia. People outside of Monrovia had no influence over the generals on the ground on both sides.

Our interests? Well, if preventing another Rwandan-scale massacre of helpless civilians was not enough, along with preventing regional instability from spreading further, there was the interest of seeing that Liberia did not become another criminal state supporting terrorists. No one thought Afghanistan mattered until 9/11.

Was I going to get someone killed? The answer was quite possibly yes. I had nearly been hit with an RPG myself. Already, some of my officers had had close calls. But that is modern diplomacy, the risk comes with the job, and everyone left at the embassy was a volunteer. Anyone who wanted to go had been released. We knew what we were up against, but we were there because we believed in our mission to save lives and stabilize the country.

So I told Washington the answer was no, I was not going to close the embassy. President Bush or John Blaney could order me to do it, but otherwise I was staying. I had promised.

CHAPTER 39

After many attempts to arrive blocked by the continuing fighting, John Blaney finally returned to Monrovia later on the same day we evacuated the Americans. One of our contract helicopters flew him in from neighboring Sierra Leone.

We knew John was coming, and I was scheduled to leave on the same helicopter. I had been in Monrovia six weeks, much longer than expected. My bags were packed.

When John stepped off the helicopter, the senior staff at the embassy immediately told him they needed me to stay. There was too much going on. Losing a deputy chief of a mission they all had faith in would be a setback. We needed to consult, at the very least, for a few days to make for a smooth transition.

I was very touched and honored that they felt that way about my leadership during the crisis we had faced together. I was ready to continue to do whatever was needed.

I also felt like Liberia had a hold on me and was never going to let go until it had figured out a way to get me killed. Every time it seemed that things had gone as bad as they could, it always got worse. Every time I thought I saw a way out, the door slammed in my face.

John looked at me and said, "Will you stay?"

I carried my suitcase back to the house and headed to my office.

John and I conferred over the next few days on the situation and what had transpired in his absence, as well as my read of the current state of affairs. Almost none of it was news to him. He had kept up on

GUARDIANS OF THE GRAIL

the latest events, and had been at a number of peace conferences trying to bring the warring parties together.

Almost as soon as he arrived, John went to pay a call on Charles Taylor, where Taylor once again hinted at U.S. embassy complicity in plotting against him. That was when John point blank told him, "If we wanted you dead, you'd be dead."

John was good, and he had guts.

John would have been happy to keep me on as his DCM, but when Washington heard I had not returned as planned, he was ordered to send me back. The Office of West African Affairs was already understaffed, and with the continuing problems in Liberia as well as in neighboring Ivory Coast, the staff was close to the breaking point handling it all. Besides, the pressure was also still on to get the staff size down even more, and sending me back at least helped John to meet that demand. So, five days later, I did catch a supply helicopter back to Freetown.

It was hard to say goodbye. In six weeks, we had done more and risked more than most colleagues do in a lifetime spent working together. I felt guilty leaving them. There would be more attacks on the city. We all knew it, and I would not be there to share in the danger.

On the other hand, I would be lying if I said I was not glad to get the hell out. It was not that I enjoyed risking my life. I am not the kind of guy who goes bungee jumping or mountain climbing or parachuting out of airplanes because I get a thrill out of risking my life. I do not. It scares the hell out me. I do it when I have to because it's my job.

So I shook hands and got on that great big blue Russian helicopter, felt the bird rattle as the blades rotated faster and it slowly rose into the air, and then with a rush dashed out to sea, rising quickly. I gazed out of the window at the embassy compound, watching it grow smaller until it faded from sight. I do not ever expect to see it again.

159

CHAPTER 40

And then another attack rained down on Monrovia. The rebels did regroup after their first assault, and the fighting resumed as fierce as before.

Again, to my astonishment, they easily swept across the bridge onto Bushrod Island, penetrating even deeper into the port this time.

And then, equally miraculously, Taylor's forces once again rallied and pushed the rebels back.

When I returned to Washington, I had no chance to rest and recuperate. The Office of West African Affairs (AF/W) was short-staffed, and because the rebels had attacked Monrovia again, the Assistant Secretary of State for African Affairs, Walter Kansteiner, called me on the Saturday I returned to ask what I thought about the situation. I told him that the mission needed all the support we could provide, and we needed to resume a twenty-four-hour Liberia task force to stay in constant touch with the embassy. Walter agreed, and I went back to working twelve-hour shifts that very day.

Michael Arietti, the new director of AF/W, and I convinced Walter Kansteiner that John Blaney needed our support. We needed U.S. troops on the ground in Liberia to stabilize the situation and stop the killing. We knew that such a U.S. intervention would be welcomed by Liberians in exactly the manner the Bush Administration had told us we would be welcomed into Iraq. Liberians love America in a unique way, as no other people on Earth love the U.S., and often talk of themselves as the fifty-first state, having been partially settled by freed American slaves. They desperately wanted us to come in, and both the rebels and Taylor's men respected and feared us, and for good reason. Their forces, as described, were little more than armed mobs. They were no match for any kind of disciplined, well equipped army, let alone the kind of superior force the United States can field.

Together, we convinced Colin Powell that it was time for a U.S. intervention in Liberia.

First of all, it was manageable. We could do the job, and it would not take more than about 5,000 troops.

Second, we could do it with few, if any, casualties, and it would not cost us much; hopefully nothing in lives and little in treasure.

Third, it would save lives. In fact, it could well prevent another massacre on the scale of Rwanda, which we said we would never let happen again.

Fourth, it would prevent Liberia from becoming another failed state, another magnet for drug lords and terrorists to not only destabilize all of West Africa, but from which they could and would threaten American interests, as well.

Fifth, Kofi Annan, the U.N. Secretary General, supported the effort and the U.N. promised that it would take over the peacekeeping mission from us in three to four months, and after that the U.S. could pull its troops out.

So we had a plan and an exit strategy, and one that would work.

Last, it would make the U.S. look good on the world stage. George Bush said that he wanted to get rid of "bad men" and wanted to support democracy everywhere in the world. This would prove that this commitment was serious. The very fact that our primary motivation for mounting an intervention was humanitarian, and not for oil or geopolitical gain, and that we did it in cooperation with allies in the U.N. and West Africa, would enhance our reputation of wanting to make the world a better place. Certainly, Charles Taylor had killed almost as many people and inflicted as much misery on his country as Saddam Hussein.

We laid all this out for Colin Powell, and I drafted briefing memos for him to use in meetings with the president and his senior advisors, including Vice President Cheney and Secretary of Defense Rumsfeld, two of the geniuses who got us into Iraq.

From discussions I had with people who were at the meetings, I was told that Cheney, and especially Rumsfeld, wanted nothing to do with Liberia.

Charles Taylor being a "bad man" was no reason to commit U.S. troops. Promoting democracy in Africa was not in our national interest. Liberia becoming a failed state did not concern them. Humanitarian issues? It was Africa.

Worst of all to me, and most maddening, was that I am told Rumsfeld commented that we had no exit strategy. He did not want to get pulled into a conflict in Africa and be stuck there.

No exit strategy? Suddenly Don Rumsfeld was wrapped around the axle about the possibility of getting stuck in a war, and this master tactician accused the State Department of not having an exit plan when it had warned *him* that he had no exit strategy for Iraq; this same Don Rumsfeld who then dismissed the State Department as a bunch of whining namby-pambies for worrying about such things as exit strategies.

We *had* an exit strategy. U.N. Secretary General Kofi Annan had committed the U.N. to follow our lead and take over the peacekeeping mission, permitting us to leave.

So there was meeting after meeting after meeting. At each one, Cheney or Rumsfeld or someone else raised an objection, and we would have to (often I had to) draft a new position paper to counter the new bogus issue; then a new meeting had to be scheduled, which took time, and when the meeting took place, a new objection was invented.

In the meantime, Rumsfeld was doing everything he could to force John Blaney in Liberia to close the embassy. "It's too dangerous," I am told he said. "We should not have an embassy there at all." Then, to make it even more dangerous, he withdrew the Navy SEAL team. Without the protection of the SEALs, he thought John would be forced to close.

But John did not close. The rebels came at Monrovia two more times, and people died as the Administration dithered. Rumsfeld and Cheney could not order John to close the embassy, only Colin Powell or the president could do that, and to their credit, they would not.

While people died, John did what he could with bluff and guts to negotiate an end to the war. Rumsfeld was finally ordered by President Bush to send a navy ship to Liberia, one headed back from Iraq, to support the mission. When it finally arrived, it only sent about fifty men into the capital, and then quickly pulled them back.

In the fighting, mortars were now routinely landing in and around our compound. Liberian employees of the embassy were killed, although no Americans died. Average Liberian citizens became so frustrated with our inaction that they dumped the bodies of the murdered in front of the embassy. When John went out for meetings, at times he had to step over the dead. He was getting precious little support from Washington, and the burden of the losses at the embassy rested on his shoulders. The bodies of the innocent killed in the fighting littered his front steps. I knew what he was going through, and I hated that as hard as I tried to support him, as hard as we all tried in the Africa Bureau, there was almost nothing we could give to help him in his cause except our own praise and hard work. But in the end, that came to very little.

Not that there wasn't incredible absurdity coming from inside the State Department, as well. I remember a meeting discussing sending American military peacekeepers into Liberia, and one department head announced that he would not clear on any such thing. The U.N. had arms sanctions on Liberia, and it would be a violation of international law for American troops to enter the country armed.

I looked at him thunderstruck. They would be part, I pointed out, of a U.N. peacekeeping mission. A mission that Kofi Annan, the Secretary General of the U.N., had personally asked us to take on as soon as we could get there.

That did not matter, he announced. We could not violate U.N. sanctions, and he for one would not stand for it.

People were dying, I said. The sanctions were to keep Charles Taylor from getting weapons. What we were proposing would in no way violate the sanctions on Liberia. We were not supplying arms to Liberia, but carrying them on a U.N. peacekeeping mission.

He folded his arms and told us none of that mattered. We could not violate the sanctions. Until the sanctions were dropped, the State Department could not support the commitment of U.S. troops.

Dropping the sanctions would have given Charles Taylor free rein to buy cheaper arms on the open market, helping him to kill more people.

I have seldom known such idiocy.

Despite this, John pushed on, almost single-handedly, but with the full backing of Colin Powell and, to his credit, President Bush. He met with Taylor. He spoke to the rebel commanders. He pressed, he threatened, he bluffed and he cajoled. It is a classic example of one man making a difference, because somehow, in the end, he succeeded.

Even at the end, the Pentagon tried to block him. When he had finally brokered an agreement to end the fighting and for Taylor to leave the country, the agreement had to be signed by the leading rebel commander, General Cobra. A stone-cold killer if ever there was one.

As John was moving in a convoy to meet with General Cobra, he received a call from the office of General James Jones, the Supreme Commander of the United States European Command, with a message that John was ordered to stop and return to the embassy immediately. It was too dangerous to cross the battle lines to meet with Cobra. He would not only be putting himself at risk, he would be putting the entire embassy at risk. He was forbidden to go.

John said he understood, but there was just one problem. He did not work for the Pentagon. He hung up and he ended the war. He personally saved the lives of tens of thousands of people.

Two years later, I would see John again. We were both attending the swearing-in ceremony for the man who would replace him as the U.S. ambassador to Liberia. At a small party afterwards in our office, held to celebrate John's retirement and the new ambassador's assignment, we talked. John admitted that he felt like a man who had been running at ninety miles an hour for the last three years and he had just sailed over a cliff. He was not sure what to do with himself.

I told him I understood completely. That was how I'd felt upon returning from Liberia after only six weeks. I didn't know how he managed three years. We then shared a few memories of what it had been like to be there under fire.

Like me, John had a lot of guilt. He told me about stepping over the bodies of women and children thrown down in front of the embassy gate. He spoke of the wasted lives he had not been able to save, and I saw tears come to his eyes. He told me about the Liberian national employees who died at the embassy, and how that would forever haunt him.

It infuriates me that the man had received so little recognition for what he accomplished, and I told him so, and I reminded him of the thousands of people who were alive because of him. "We could not save them all," I said, "but we saved so very many."

He nodded, and then he looked me in the eyes and he said, "Chris, I want to thank you again for keeping my embassy open."

Coming from him, that meant more to me than anything anyone has ever said to me before or since.

John and I were never great power brokers in Washington, and John, in particular, did what he could without much help, and sometimes even heavy opposition, from those at the top. I am reminded of a cultural icon, the wizard Gandalf the Grey, who, when asked why he had included a small and seemingly insignificant hobbit in his quest to kill a dragon, says, "I don't know. Saruman believes it is only great power that can hold evil in check, but that is not what I have found. I've found it is the small everyday deeds of ordinary folk that keep the darkness at bay... small acts of kindness, and love. Why Bilbo Baggins? Perhaps it is because I am afraid... and he gives me courage."

John certainly is the kind of man who should give us all courage.

CHAPTER 41

During my tour in AF/W, I watched from inside the State Department as we prepared for the second Iraq war, and despite the Administration's protestations early on that it had not made up its mind to go to war, it was obvious it had made exactly that decision.

I was horrified. We should only fight justifiable wars we have a reasonably good chance of winning, or because we have no other choice and our very national existence depends upon the outcome.

None of that was true in Iraq.

A great deal of excellent analysis has been written and said about the fiasco that was our adventure in Iraq, so I'll only discuss my personal experience of it.

Saddam Hussein was no "imminent" threat to the U.S. Yes, he had been evading sanctions and was living very well himself, but his country and his military were seriously weakened. He had not used weapons of mass destruction against us in the first Gulf War, and he was far weaker at the start of the second.

As for the nuclear threat he posed, against which, we were told by Dick Cheney and Condi Rice, we must act before there was a mushroom cloud over America: from the limited intelligence I had seen, I knew that threat was highly questionable. First, it was obvious from intelligence reports I saw that the aluminum tubes that were supposedly to be used by Saddam for uranium processing could not be used for that purpose. They were intended for building artillery, and were not of sufficient strength to be used in centrifuges to process enriched uranium.

Second, I knew the reports that Saddam had tried to buy uranium from Niger were also false. Niger is in West Africa and one of the countries in my portfolio. I knew in detail about the uranium operation there.

We had seen repeated reports that Saddam was trying to buy uranium from Niger, but when examined closely those reports always turned out to be based on forged documents, and poor quality forgeries at that. We discovered con artists created them to sell to journalists looking for a hot story.

The same set of forgeries set off multiple alarms. First, our analysts saw them and raised a red flag only to discover the documents were fakes. Then another nation's intelligence service contacted us to say they had discovered hot evidence Saddam was trying to buy uranium from Niger and we got concerned, only to discover that they had independently obtained the same forgeries we had already seen. This happened several times, creating the false impression of multiple independently verified reports.

Furthermore, when we looked into the possibility of Saddam getting uranium from Niger, we came to understand just how hard it would be. In fact, it would have been impossible for us not to discover it. This is because the mining of uranium in Niger is not controlled by the government of Niger, but by a consortium of international countries led by the French, who mine the uranium for their own use and not for sale on the open market. The French, not the Nigerians, would absolutely have known that a large amount of the ore they had mined was going to some unknown destination.

Before the war started I received a request for information from other divisions in the State Department about the possibility of uranium being sold by Niger to Iraq. In no uncertain terms my office stated that these reports were false, pointing out that they were all based on documents we knew to be fabrications and that the logistics of such a sale made it virtually impossible.

We were told that the White House wanted all available reports on possible Iraqi efforts to obtain uranium, no matter how unlikely. We provided the information, clearly stating it to be false and why.

A few weeks later, in his State of the Union address, President Bush accused Saddam Hussein of trying to buy uranium from an African country and made this accusation a centerpiece of his justification for going to war.

I almost fell over. We were going to war based on intelligence we knew was bogus.

Did George Bush lie about the intelligence on Iraq to convince America to go to war? He certainly didn't tell the truth, but he may not have known what he claimed was not true. I think there were people in his Administration who knew better; in my opinion, Dick Cheney primarily among them. He set up his own intelligence unit, from what I have read, and he must have known how weak so much of the information they used really was, or at least his not knowing was willful. But that, I admit, is speculation.

The real question in my mind is why George Bush wanted to go to war with Iraq so badly that he mobilized the White House to collect what he needed to justify his fiasco.

Bush was surrounded by the infamous Neo-cons who were disastrously ignorant and misinformed about the Middle East and what we were walking into. These folks were the Keystone Kops of international affairs and their ideas and actions would actually have been comic except for the enormous amount of death, destruction and harm they caused. They got *everything* wrong. We would be welcomed as liberators. Iraqi oil would pay for the war. The new government would be a democratic model the Middle East would follow. And so on.

But what they did do successfully was convince George Bush that Iraq would be a walk in the park, one that would forever change the face of the Middle East and remake it in our image. It was a concept of colossal stupidity and arrogance that could only have been hatched by people who understood nothing of the region or its history. Yet, like many simplistic and horribly wrong-headed ideas, it had siren-like appeal for the uninformed.

CHAPTER 42

In 2005, the State Department opened a new Consulate in Juba, South Sudan. Serving there was a one-year assignment in one of the most isolated places on Earth.

South Sudan has a long and troubled history, situated in one of the worst international communities imaginable. The north of Sudan is essentially Muslim and Arab, while the south is largely Christian and African. Almost from the independence of Sudan from Great Britain in 1953, the northern ruling elite largely marginalized the south. Furthermore, the north attempted to impose Islam on the south, which the south resisted. Frankly, given the ethnic, religious and cultural differences between the two regions, the south should never have been a part of Sudan, another example of bad British mapmaking. Syria, Jordan, Iraq, India, Pakistan—there is a long list of hell and death wrought by the foolish policies of the post-Empire Brits. Unsurprisingly, civil war broke out in Sudan in 1962. After years of fighting, a temporary peace was reached in 1972. The agreement provided for religious and some cultural and political autonomy for southern Sudan.

It did not last. In 1983, President Gaafar Nimeiry declared Sudan to be an Islamic state and he terminated the 1972 accords granting the south religious autonomy. Civil war resumed and raged until 2005. During this time, out of a southern population of about eight million, over two million southerners died and over four million were dislocated from their homes, some of them repeatedly. Many people today have heard of the conflict in Darfur in western Sudan. About six times as many people died in the fighting in southern Sudan than have been killed in Darfur.

During this long war, the north made almost no investment in the south. When I arrived in Juba in January of 2008, there were five miles of paved roads in all of southern Sudan. There was no public school system. There were almost no medical facilities anywhere. Illiteracy ran at 85% or more, and everyone who had an education got it by going to school in another country. The south could not feed itself, not because of a lack of arable land but because farmers had been dislocated so often that many had given up trying to raise crops. Even those who grew crops could not get them to markets because there were no roads. Despite great mineral wealth, including oil, southern Sudan was one of the poorest regions on Earth. What mineral extraction there was went to the benefit of the north, mostly in the form of oil taken from oil fields located in southern Sudan.

In the meantime, Khartoum was transformed. When I had arrived in Khartoum in 1993, it was the shabbiest city I had ever seen until I saw Monrovia under President Taylor. Few roads were paved, few cars traveled them, the stores were mostly empty and there were few modern facilities. When I arrived in 2008, Khartoum had transformed into a modern city of bustling traffic on good roads, new construction underway everywhere, modern supermarkets selling all manner of luxury goods, a modern airport and plenty of schools and modern medical facilities. These were mostly financed with oil money stolen from the south, and from which the south received no benefit other than death and destruction at the hands of a brutal military machine also largely financed with oil money.

Southerners were an abused people, denied even their most basic human rights and slaughtered, brutalized and neglected.

But the story of American involvement in this conflict was again an example of the best of us. We kept pressure on Khartoum over the years to end the war while we supported southerners with food aid. In 2005, in concert with our European allies but most especially the British and Norwegians, we negotiated a peace treaty called the Comprehensive Peace Agreement, or CPA. The south was again granted autonomy from Khartoum, with a six-year interim period before southern Sudan was to hold a referendum in 2011 on whether to declare itself an independent nation. The interim period was to give peace a chance and see if the two sides could reconcile their differences and remain a united nation.

The job I took was to be the Consul General of the U.S. Consulate in Juba. That meant I was in charge of the mission, reporting to our embassy in Khartoum 700 miles away.

I arrived in Khartoum after a two-day journey on the evening of January 1, 2008. The embassy expediters who greeted me immediately informed me that Islamic extremists had just assassinated a thirty-three-year-old American diplomat, John Granville.

It was the perfect assignment for me: dangerous, little chance for success, isolated and almost certain to explode.

CHAPTER 43

At the signing of the Comprehensive Peace Agreement in 2005, Juba, the capital of southern Sudan, was a government garrison town of about 50,000 people. When I arrived in 2008, it had grown to about 400,000. By the time I left in 2012 after my second assignment, it was pushing a million.

The compound that was to become our Consulate was originally part of a United States Agency for International Development (USAID) facility built to manage the flow of foreign food aid to southern Sudan during the civil war. After a 1989 coup by Islamists that overthrew the elected government in Khartoum, relations with the U.S. grew increasingly strained. In August of 1992, government forces invaded the USAID Juba compound, arrested four of our local southern Sudanese employees and executed them as "spies" without cause or justification in a move typical of the nastiness of the government in Khartoum. We closed the USAID office as a result and rented the compound out to the Red Cross for a dollar a year until 2005, when we opened the Consulate and took the property back.

Our compound had four three-bedroom houses, a guesthouse with several bedrooms, a restaurant and a gym with a swimming pool. The water in the swimming pool was green and populated by frogs and mosquitoes, the dilapidated houses were crawling with insects and vermin, including the occasional black mamba, one of the deadliest snakes in the world. Juba has every dangerous tropical disease known to man, including cerebral malaria that can be fatal within forty-eight hours of the onset of symptoms. When I arrived to take over the mission, my staff consisted of seventeen American officers, most of them working for USAID. For the State Department, there was just my deputy and me.

Juba is a dangerous place, not because the people are hostile, but because they are so poor and guns are so readily available. If guns make you safe, southern Sudan would be the safest place on Earth; of course it's not.

Americans are loved in southern Sudan due to our long support for its people, particularly with food aid, during their decades-long struggle for independence and for our role in brokering the peace agreement that ended the war, but that did not make us safe.

In 2008, southern Sudan was completely a cash economy. Credit cards and bank checks were useless. Juba was full of international public and private aid groups doing their best to bring assistance to the region, but to pay staff and purchase supplies required that everyone keep large sums of cash on hand. Men with guns quickly learned that if you squeezed an aid group, money came out, so nighttime compound invasions by men with AK-47s became a common event.

This required that my U.S. staff live on our heavily guarded compound, that we have a curfew of midnight to be home and that we travel everywhere in armored vehicles.

I was the only Consul General in the world who shared his residence with roommates. Every bedroom space was needed, and so my female deputy had one bedroom in our house, my male defense attaché had another and I had the third. We shared the living room and kitchen. It was like being back in college.

In addition, we had no office space so our offices were our bedrooms.

We generated our own electricity because there was no dependable power grid and we drilled our own wells for water because there was no reliable waterworks. Our generators were overworked and failed often. The water pumps overheated and once caught fire. The American contractor who ran our support services lived in a tent.

Our mission was to strengthen relations with the embryonic new government of southern Sudan, preserve the peace, turn a guerrilla southern army into a disciplined national defense force, help build education and primary healthcare networks, promote agricultural development, help build infrastructure (including roads) and, last but not least, promote democratic development. Short on educated managerial talent, southern Sudan was starting from almost zero in all these areas. As I said, I had seventeen people working out of their bedrooms and we needed more staff for this very ambitious program, but we had no room to house them. To make up for the lack of staff, we worked long hours seven days a week.

This was *Indiana-Jones*-style expeditionary American diplomacy on the ragged edge of the universe in 2008. So much for the public image of U.S. diplomats in pinstriped suits drinking martinis and living in high style.

CHAPTER 44

The greatest threat to the future of southern Sudan is not from Khartoum (although they do present a threat and seize every opportunity available to try to undermine the south), but from internal divisions. Southern Sudan is composed of a tapestry of about sixty-four different tribal groups, each with distinct traditions, languages and aspirations. The largest tribe is the Dinka, but even they break down into many sub-clans that are often at odds with each other. The Dinka make up about 35-40% of the population. Then there are the Nuer, the Murle, the Shiluk, the Bari, the Acholi and on and on.

One of the reasons the civil war lasted as long as it did was that, over the years, Khartoum successfully set the various tribal groups against each other in a constantly shifting web of alliances and betrayals.

Perhaps the most symbolic illustration of the fragile state of South Sudan's unity rests in the individuals who, when I was there, occupied the offices of the president and vice president of South Sudan.

Salva Kiir Mayardit was, and still is at the time of this writing, the president of South Sudan. He is a Dinka. The Dinka are renowned for being tall, and he is no exception. You may remember the NBA player Manute Bol, who was a Dinka from southern Sudan and who stood seven feet seven inches tall. I am five feet eleven and many Dinka women towered over me.

Dr. John Garang, also a Dinka, for decades led the fight against the government in Khartoum and briefly became the president of southern

Sudan, but died in a somewhat suspicious helicopter crash soon after the signing of the Comprehensive Peace Accord in 2005.[2]

Dr. Garang is thought of as the George Washington of South Sudan, and his memory is deeply venerated. His ambition was not to break away from Sudan, but to become the president of a united Sudan. A southern Christian, he believed (and perhaps rightly so) that the Arab elites who have ruled Sudan since independence are really a minority in the country and that a coalition of all the marginalized regions of Sudan could, in a free and fair election, win the presidency. That was his goal, but it was largely a goal that died with him when his helicopter went down.

I met John Garang on a few occasions when I served at our embassy in Eritrea. The Sudanese opposition had an office there that Garang sometimes visited. On one occasion, I mentioned to him that the U.S. was conducting an extensive demining program in Eritrea, which at the time was one of the most heavily mined countries in the world following their civil war with Ethiopia. It was unsafe to walk anywhere off a well-worn path for fear of blowing off a leg or worse.

Dr. Garang jovially asked me what we did with the mines we uncovered.

I said we destroyed them.

He smiled and said, "Don't do that. Give them to me. I can use them."

I laughed and said, "I'm sorry, Dr. Garang, but we only want to have to dig them up once."

Garang was also an autocrat who, I think, would have ruled with an iron fist. His rebel army was really an amalgamation of several tribal militias, each with its own leader who commanded its loyalty. After the signing of the peace treaty with Khartoum, Garang intended to create one united army in the south and crush any militia that did not agree to join it or disband. Fighting and bloodshed were expected.

Salva Kiir Mayardit is an entirely different man from Garang. Garang was well educated, with a B.A. in economics from Grinnell College in Iowa. Kiir, as he is commonly referred to, has a sixth-grade education.

---

2. You will notice that I jump between calling this region southern Sudan and South Sudan. It was southern Sudan before independence, and became the Republic of South Sudan after independence on July 9, 2011.

I do not believe it was even remotely Garang's intention for Kiir to succeed him. Garang saw Kiir, I think, as an effective military commander who did not present a threat to his leadership and never would. As mentioned earlier, many African presidents watch their backs carefully, always fearful of a coup.

But Garang died unexpectedly and Kiir, as vice president, did succeed him.

Kiir is different from Garang in other important ways. He was *not* an autocrat, at least not at the start. He reached out to all the independent militia forces and found ways to bring them into the national army. This often required giving the leadership of those militias high-level government or military posts they did not merit, but by doing so Kiir kept the peace.

Kiir's Cabinet included somewhere around thirty ministers when it should probably have been seven and not more than ten. But given the need to grant prestigious titles to so many military and tribal leaders in order to keep the nation unified, he had no choice but to build a big tent. As Lyndon Johnson is so famously reported to have said, "It's better to have your enemies inside the tent pissing out than outside the tent pissing in."

When I was in southern Sudan, Kiir governed by consensus. Every Friday was Cabinet meeting day, when almost every major decision of the government was put to a vote and Kiir nearly always accepted the majority decision. This strategy brought along the military and tribal leadership he depended upon to preserve unity.

The few instances where Kiir did not follow the majority vote involved provocations by Khartoum before independence in 2011, when the north carried out attacks on disputed border areas. Many in the south wanted to retaliate and war fever ran high. Kiir resisted it. He wanted to give the government in Khartoum no excuse for calling off the referendum on independence. He rightly and cleverly met provocations with a calm determination to avoid conflict. It worked.

For several years Kiir did a remarkable job of preserving southern unity given the fragile internal political situation. Unfortunately, it was not to last.

The problem Kiir's accommodation approach created was the high cost of corruption. Too many in his Cabinet saw the government as a personal money spigot. But Kiir could not fire them from the very real fear that they might go into the bush and lead a revolt against his government, which they often threatened to do when they did not get their way, and which did happen more than once. So, pay them off and keep the peace, or hold them to account and watch the country come apart at the seams with tribal conflict. I did not envy Kiir his job.

Kiir's vice president at the time I was there was Riek Machar. That he occupied that position for several years was a tribute to his ambition, intelligence and ability. He is a Nuer with a PhD from the University of Bradford and he spent much of the war years switching sides, sometimes fighting Garang and Kiir on the side of Khartoum. In one instance during the war, when he was allied with Khartoum, his forces are reported to have slaughtered up to 10,000 Dinka. Toward the end of the war he rejoined Garang, who had to take him back because he needed him as a prominent leader of the Nuer, the largest tribe after the Dinka.

I met Machar on many occasions, and he is an oddly charismatic character. Although a Christian, he has at least three wives, which is fairly common for Christians in South Sudan. Early on, one of his wives was a very attractive young British national named Emma McCune. She died in a car accident in Nairobi in 1993, when was twenty-nine years old and pregnant. There is a book written about her by journalist Deborah Scroggins titled *Emma's War*, in which Machar figures prominently. I highly recommend it.

Today, one of his three wives is an American. She came to southern Sudan with her missionary husband, met Machar, fell in love, divorced her husband and married him. As I said, the man has charisma.

To say that Kiir and Machar do not like each other is like saying the Hatfields and the McCoys had a small feud. Besides the bitterness over Machar's actions during the war and his attacks on Dinka, Machar wants Kiir's job and Kiir knows it. I believe the Dinka simply would not stand for it, but I know for a fact Machar wants to be president, and it is this ambition that was to be South Sudan's undoing.

There are two primary lifestyles among the tribes of South Sudan. There are the tribes of farmers and then of cattle herders. Loyalty and identity are strongly anchored in tribal affiliation. A sense of national identity is weak in many, if not most, parts of the country due to the weak infrastructure, which allows for little travel or exchange between regions or communication with the central government. Juba, the capital, is a long way away and what happens there seems to hardly touch the lives of the rest of the country.

But the real heart of the problem was those damn cows.

For centuries, cattle herding has been a predominant means of making a living in what is today South Sudan. Stealing cattle from neighboring tribes is a long tradition and is often a rite of passage required for a boy to become recognized as a man. Until the modern era, raiding parties were small and armed with bows and spears. A few cows were stolen, every once in a while someone was killed, but women, children and the elderly were not harmed.

Now everyone is heavily armed with automatic weapons that dramatically increase the killings. Raiding parties have grown in size, sometimes thousands of cows are taken and women, children and the elderly are often targeted. More than that, whole villages are sometimes attacked and burned, often destroying new infrastructure improvements including schools and clinics.

The odd thing is that the cows are seldom used for productive purposes. They are not often eaten, there is no cheese industry and the hides are seldom used. Essentially, the cows are a form of currency. Without a banking system, especially in the rural areas, a man's wealth is not measured in dollars or South Sudanese pounds, but in cows. When a man wants to marry, he pays the bride price in cows. The price depends on a number of factors, including the prestige or wealth of the bride's family, the attractiveness of the bride, the prestige of the groom's family and so forth. In my experience, the price tended to run between 100 to 200 cows.

I once traveled with a delegation to a remote area, and a member of our group was a rather attractive young blonde woman named Sara. As the senior representative of the United States on this mission, a prominent chief offered me 600 cows for this woman. I cannot remember how many wives he already had, but it was at least three, so Sara would become wife number four. Had I accepted the offer, it would have made me a wealthy man even by Western standards.

Naturally, I had to politely decline by telling the chief Sara was already married to me (a white lie, but a way out that did not give offense), and forever afterwards the woman was known at the Consulate as Sara 600.

Today the cows are really a curse. There are too many of them for the available pastureland, they are not very productive and they are a leading source of deadly conflict between rival raiding parties. Animosities and grudges that run back centuries over cattle raids and murders now explode into genocidal massacres. The government of South Sudan has trouble containing the violence because there are few roads, which makes moving police and troops to constantly changing conflict zones difficult and time consuming; during the rainy season such travel can be impossible except by helicopters, which are in short supply. Further, the loyalty of sections of the army is questionable because tribal affiliations can mean that some troops will not fight and others might actually support the raiding community.

A prominent South Sudanese general once told me that the best thing that could happen for the good of the nation would be to kill all the cows. Where there are farming communities, there is little violence. Further, the cows are destructive to farming. They have to be constantly moved to follow the yearly rains that support pastureland, and farmers must go to great lengths to build natural fences to keep the cows out of their crops. They do not dare kill invading cows out of fear of retaliation by the heavily armed herders.

The government in Khartoum often supports this fighting by supplying arms and ammunition to the combatants (sometimes even arming both sides) in order to destabilize South Sudan and weaken the government. An internally weak South Sudan presents less of a threat to Khartoum over border and resource issues (the border with Sudan remains largely unsettled). In return, the government in South Sudan supports rebel groups in Sudan, hoping to topple that government.

After one particularly troubling episode of violence between Nuer and Murle raiders that destroyed villages, killed hundreds of people including women and children and which resulted in the theft of thousands of cattle, I traveled with the head of the United Nations peacekeeping operation to the affected area. The U.N. mission is called the United Nations Mission to the Republic of South Sudan, or UNMISS, and was headed at that time by Hilde Johnson, a Norwegian. It is the largest U.N. peacekeeping presence in the world.

We first flew by helicopter into a Murle village and met with the tribal leadership. The elders told us how unhappy they were that they

GUARDIANS OF THE GRAIL

had seen little in the way of development benefits from the U.N., the U.S. or the central government.

We pointed out that a clinic and school had been built in their town, but raiders burned them to the ground. If they wanted development, they needed to put an end to cattle raiding by both sides. If they could not stop their constant feuding, what was the use of building infrastructure that would just be destroyed? They must, we said, let go of old grudges and make peace with their neighbors. When their youth assembled to raid, they must put a stop to it. Then there could be schools and roads and clinics and development. If the violence did not stop, on the other hand, none of those things would come to them and the future would be the same as the past.

The elders allowed that there was truth in that, but those damn Nuer could not be trusted. Every leader had a story of how they had lost a relative, and by God they were going to get their own back from those sons of bitches.

When we visited the Nuer village, we gave and heard the same messages.

You cannot make people behave. They have to want to.

CHAPTER 45

I always thought Riek Machar, the then-vice president of South Sudan, was a scoundrel, but I liked him anyway. It was hard not to, and just meeting him you would never think he had been a warlord. He is affable, funny and approachable. I sometimes had to limit the number of times I met him because of his rivalry with President Kiir, who might have begun to think I was supporting Machar to replace him.

On one occasion I met with President Kiir, and he was so angry at Machar's most recent attempts to do an end run around his office in negotiating a peace settlement with the government in Khartoum, that his hands shook as he discussed it. Keeping Machar contained was like trying to hang on to an electric eel.

Although a Nuer, Machar is every bit as big as a Dinka, and he has a pronounced gap between his two front teeth that is on prominent display whenever he smiles, which is often.

After the end of the war for independence, Machar dedicated himself to becoming a peacemaker. It was a strategy to enable him to eventually replace Kiir. Machar wanted to put his reputation as a warlord who killed thousands of Dinka behind him, and replace it with a new persona as a peacemaker who could bind the country together. In my opinion, he was overly optimistic about the Dinka's willingness to forgive and forget.

In 2008 and 2009, Machar headed an effort to end the insurgency known as the Lord's Resistance Army, led by the indicted war criminal Joseph Kony.

Kony is pure, brutal, your worst nightmare, you hope there is a hell so he can go to it, unforgiving evil.

The nightmare that is Joseph Kony began in northern Uganda, which borders South Sudan. Northern Uganda is composed largely of the Acholi, a cattle herding tribe. In the late 1980s, the government in Uganda persecuted this community, killing many of their cattle and creating unrest that spawned a number of armed rebel groups. One of these was taken over by Joseph Kony, who renamed it (or misnamed it) the Lord's Resistance Army, or LRA.

Kony masks himself as a Christian religious leader whose program is based on the Ten Commandments. Ironically, Rush Limbaugh once asserted that the effort to try to capture or kill Kony was part of a program by the Obama Administration to support Muslim extremists in their efforts to destroy and persecute Christians. Of course, Limbaugh had no clue what he was talking about. Kony came from a Christian community but he perpetrates his atrocities largely against other Christians.

The reality is there is not a single one of the Ten Commandments Kony has not routinely shattered. Over the last twenty years, at least 20,000 have been murdered by his group and up to two million have fled or been forced into Internally Displaced Person (IDP) and refugee camps.

The following is part of a report describing Kony by the group Invisible Children.

> Soon after Joseph Kony assumed management of the group, he changed the name to the Lord's Resistance Army, or LRA. Joseph Kony wasn't able to maintain the group's numbers or regional support, so he started stealing food and abducting children to fill the ranks of his army. Subsequently, he lost any remaining regional support. What had started out as a rebel movement to end the oppression of the north became an oppression of the north in itself.
>
> Joseph Kony's tactics were and remain brutal. He often forced children to kill their parents or siblings with machetes or blunt tools. He abducted girls to be sex slaves for his officers. He brainwashed and indoctrinated the children with his lies and manipulated them with his claim of spiritual powers.
>
> At the height of the conflict in Uganda, children "night commuted." That is, every evening they would walk miles from their homes to the city centers. There, hundreds of children would sleep in schoolhouses, churches, or bus depots to avoid abduction by the LRA.

Kony and the LRA abducted more than 30,000 children in northern Uganda.

Forcing a child to kill his own parents or siblings is a diabolically shrewd way to break a child's bonds to his community and force the child to, ironically, look to his captors as surrogate parents. It is sick and immoral but it works. A child, emotionally crippled by what he has done, psychologically seeks to form new attachments. Children have an overwhelming need to have a parent figure. Those children who refused to murder their parents were themselves butchered by Kony along with their parents in front of other children who were about to be required to perform the same sick task. This resulted in instances of parents begging their own children to murder them, knowing that they would be killed no matter what happened and wanting their children at least to survive.

Eventually Kony was driven out of Uganda, and today he operates in parts of South Sudan, Congo and the Central African Republic, encompassing an area about the size of California. His original rationale for creating his rebel army is now gone, since he is no longer engaging the government of Uganda in an attempt to overthrow it. His continuing tactics of theft, murder and abduction are simply a means of perpetuating a perverted cult following that recognizes him as god.

Kony operates in some of the most isolated and difficult terrain to be found anywhere in the world. His forces today are estimated to be only about 200 fighters. While Kony is crazy, he is a master tactician. He divides his "army" into smaller units of ten to thirty fighters who operate largely independently, but who periodically reunite to provide supplies to, and receive instructions from, Kony.

In 2008, I joined the attempt to negotiate an end to the fighting. Timothy Shortley was appointed by the African Bureau in the State Department to lead our effort to coordinate with Riek Machar's mediation effort, and Tim was an able diplomat. His home base was in Washington, DC, however, and since I was stationed in Juba as the leader of our mission there, we worked closely together so that when he could not attend meetings I could carry on in his place.

The effort started in 2006 with the signing of a cease-fire agreement. The cease-fire had its ups and downs, but Kony and his forces finally settled in eastern Congo near the border with southern Sudan. Part of the agreement provided for the LRA to be supplied with food and medicines. I spoke to Machar about this a few times, and his justification for providing such aid was that it kept Kony's forces in one place, stopped the senseless killings and the abductions of children, and it removed the need for the LRA to raid villages to acquire the supplies they required.

When I arrived in Juba in January of 2008, the negotiations were in high gear again. Many were optimistic that they could succeed in ending the blight of the LRA. I was not. The reason was the International Criminal Court, or ICC. It had indicted Kony for war crimes, and as long as Kony feared being sent to The Hague to stand trial, I believed he would never come out of the bush, with the result that an ever-increasing number of innocent men, women and children would continue to die because of elite Western do-gooders who are more interested in satisfying their moral outrage that justice be done than they are in saving lives and children.

Just as with Liberian President Charles Taylor and the Special Court for Sierra Leone, these Western elites will tell you that demanding accountability will save lives in the long run. If tyrants know that the mighty hand of justice will eventually punish crimes against humanity, future acts of horror will not be perpetrated out of fear of being held answerable.

Nonsense. People like Kony and Taylor never think about being held accountable; half the time they are so psychotic they don't even see what they are doing as wrong. If you ask Kony, and we did, he will tell you he is the victim of a brutal regime in Uganda and is the champion of his people.

And so these righteous men and women of the ICC, whose children are in no danger of being abducted, whose wives and daughters are in no danger of being raped and enslaved, and who themselves are at no risk of being brutally murdered, all sleep well at night knowing that they are the potent instruments of justice.

My view of indicting people like Kony is that if you cannot arrest them, mind your own business. You are not helping with indictments that cannot be enforced and that only ensure the perpetrators of war crimes have no reason to stop their killing.

Do I want to see justice done to Kony? Absolutely. I would shoot the bastard in the head myself if I could, and be happy to do it. But I knew for a fact that those ICC indictments against him guaranteed he would not leave the bush and thousands of women and children would continue to suffer and die at his hands as a result. The dead are the dead, sad as that may be. I always try to see that no more bodies get added to the pile.

That said, I was willing to give peace a chance and work with Machar to see if we could coax Kony to put down his arms. Like me, Machar cared first and foremost about ending the killing.

Sadly, although Kony mostly behaved himself during the peace talks while his troops were being fed and he no longer needed to prey on the local population in Congo, he also used the break from the military pressure on him to rest and re-equip his followers.

Naturally, Joseph Kony would not come to Juba to participate in the discussions. He is a paranoid psychotic, but as is so often said, even paranoids have enemies, and as the world's most wanted war criminal he certainly had his fair share.

Instead, Kony appointed a panel of people to represent him, this delegation being led by David Matsanga, a Ugandan.

Peace talk participants included Kony's representatives, Riek Machar as the lead negotiator, U.N. Special Representative of the Secretary-General for LRA-affected areas Joaquim Chissano (also a former African head of state) and representatives of the Ugandan government, with the U.S. as an observer. We were in a delicate position. The U.S. had designated the LRA a terrorist group and our policy is not to negotiate with terrorists. So we could not publicly and officially sit on the panel. As "observers," however, we were positioned to do what we could behind the scenes, and in truth this was really a cover since we participated actively in all aspects of the talks, often taking the lead in pushing the parties to an agreement and supporting the effort financially.

Another art of diplomacy is the ability to sit at a negotiating table and listen to people say the most preposterous things imaginable while pretending to take them seriously. Public posturing is nearly always a part of the pantomime of negotiations and you cannot box people in by calling them liars. Well, most of the time you cannot.

Once again I was dancing with the devil, and for hours on end I had to listen to LRA lead spokesman David Matsanga and his group tell us that the LRA was a liberation army fighting a repressive regime in Uganda that had oppressed and abused the Acholi. Joseph Kony, they said, was a hero to his people, the only one standing up for their rights.

The reports of the abductions of children, the rape and sexual enslavement of women and the murder of thousands of innocents were all lies perpetrated by the Ugandan government to besmirch the good name of Joseph Kony.

It made me sick to hear it, but I sat through it with a poker face. In the evenings and on breaks, I often had to socialize with them, smiling and making small talk.

Machar handled the situation well, constantly steering the discussion back to focus on what Kony needed to be able to sign a permanent cessation of hostilities.

Naturally, Matsanga spoke of justice for the Acholi people, which included the need for the government to pay reparations for the Acholi cattle slaughtered by the government and for development assistance for northern Uganda that would include schools and clinics, blah blah blah.

After all that posturing, we then got down to brass tacks. Kony wanted the indictments by the ICC lifted. His people wanted to be appointed to high-level government positions. Kony wanted amnesty. These, of course, were the real sticking points, especially the last.

The ICC refused to lift the indictments. One way to get around that was to bring Kony to trial in Uganda using the Ugandan criminal justice system. If the ICC deemed the trials fair and competent, it would accept the verdicts and drop its international indictments.

Kony wanted to know how the trials in Uganda would be organized and what penalties he might face. It was hinted that he could be placed under house arrest on a large farm with his family, including his multiple wives. I had my doubts the ICC would accept such an outcome, and so did Kony.

The negotiating was complicated by the fact that Matsanga was scared to death of Kony. Kony had only recently murdered one of his most senior generals for pushing the peace process too vigorously. Matsanga personally appealed to me to see that he got more concessions to take to Kony. Without them he feared, with some justification, that Kony would kill him, too.

It was hard to reach Kony to discuss offers and counter offers. Kony knew that getting on a satellite phone to talk to his negotiators gave away his exact location in the bush, so Kony sent people out of his camp to remote locations to talk on the phone to deliver and collect messages. This meant days could go by while we waited for Kony to get back to us. Matsanga resisted going to see Kony personally out of fear he would not return.

A breakthrough was achieved February 3, 2008, regarding accountability and reconciliation. It was agreed that war crimes would be tried in a special section of the High Court of Uganda, bypassing the International Criminal Court. On February 22, Matsanga walked out of the talks again after his delegation was denied senior posts in the Ugandan government. Then they signed another agreement in which the Ugandan government stated that they "would be considered for government and army posts," but not automatically appointed.

Riek often kept us in session far into the early hours of the morning hammering out agreements. This is a common tactic of experienced negotiators to tire everyone out to where they will agree to almost anything if they can just go home and get some sleep. It's surprising how often it works. In this country you often see labor/corporate negotiations go on into the early hours of the morning for the same reason.

An agreement was finally reached. Kony said he would sign it. A large delegation, including representatives of the U.N., all the members of the negotiating team, the media, prominent community leaders from the Acholi and other affected tribes flew by multiple helicopters to a remote location on the border between southern Sudan and Congo. I went with them. We spent hours waiting for Kony to show. I went far enough into the jungle to cross the border so I could say I have been to Congo.

Several of Kony's heavily armed men showed up on our periphery and circled our camp: young men dressed in khaki pants and tee shirts with AK47s strapped across their backs.

Kony never showed. The agreement was never signed. Just as I expected, as long as the ICC indictments stood, Kony would get cold feet.

Riek Machar wanted to let Kony stay where he was and continue to feed and clothe his troops in the hope that they would settle down, turn to farming, and keep quiet. Others wanted to go after him militarily in the hopes of capturing or killing him. Riek was adamantly opposed to that. In hindsight, Riek was right and his would have probably been the best course of action.

The following is from an Invisible Children report:

In December 2008, when it became clear that Kony wasn't going to sign the agreement, Operation Lightning Thunder was launched. It was the coordinated effort of Uganda, Democratic Republic of Congo, the Central African Republic, and Sudan, with intelligence and logistical support from the United States.

The operation failed. Joseph Kony somehow learned of the attack in the hours before the air-raid and so he was able to escape. In retribution for the attempted attack, the LRA, led by ICC-indictee Dominic Ongwen, attacked villages in the DR Congo on December 24, 2008, killing 865 civilians and abducting 160 more over the course of 2 weeks. The LRA fighters were reportedly instructed to target churches, where people would be gathered with their families for Christmas Eve services. (So much for Rush Limbaugh's assertion that we were supporting Muslims attempting to oppress LRA Christian freedom fighters.)

A year later the LRA reprised the Christmas massacres in the Makombo region in northeastern Congo as a reminder of its powers of destruction. These attacks took place over four days, from December 14-18, 2009. This time they killed 321 people and abducted 250.

Because of the remote region of the Makombo massacres in December 2009, the outside world knew nothing about the attacks until three months later. Human Rights Watch broke the news internationally on March 28, 2010.

So, the ICC and the justice-at-any-price American and European elites got their way and poor African peasants once again paid the price of their hubris with their lives and the lives of their children.

Since 2010 many, many more innocents have been abducted, murdered, dislocated and forced into sexual slavery.

The U.S., I am happy to say, is still actively engaged in special forces operations in support of local military authorities in South Sudan, Congo and Central African Republic, doing our best to bring Kony down. Kony is under a lot of pressure and his forces have been reduced, but he is, sadly, still active.

In July of 2008, the ICC again issued an unenforceable indictment, this time against the president of Sudan, Omar Hassan al-Bashir. Bashir is responsible for the deaths of hundreds of thousands of people in the western area of Sudan known as Darfur, as well as for hundreds of thousands of deaths in southern Sudan during that civil war. But once again a pointless indictment accomplished nothing but to cement Bashir in power. In a conversation with me, President Kiir once said of Bashir, "From the office to the cemetery," meaning that Bashir would never leave his hold on power until he died. The ICC guaranteed that outcome.

Bashir regularly flaunts the indictment by traveling to other African countries that, as members of the International Criminal Court, are supposed to arrest him. They don't and he loves to thumb his nose at the ICC. Many African leaders feel the court is selective in its indictments and chooses to pick on Africa because it is easy to do. They claim our war in Iraq was a war of choice based on faulty or intentionally misleading intelligence. Tens of thousands lost their lives because of it. Based on that, there are those African leaders who maintain that President Bush and Vice President Cheney are war criminals who should be indicted. It would have been political suicide for the ICC to do that, of course, which is exactly the point these Africans make.

But there is no doubt that Omar Hassan al-Bashir has murdered hundreds of thousands of people, and even if you think the ICC is not equal in its assessment of the need for justice to be done, Bashir is a killer who should never be welcomed to any country, indictment or not.

With the ICC indictments against Bashir, there is no reason for him to step down from power and every reason to remain. A successor government might well turn him over to stand trial. He will now hang on no matter what pressure is placed on him. It's the better option. And so the ICC has locked Bashir in place and defeated any future diplomatic solution to the problem of democratic development in Sudan for the foreseeable future.

Until the ICC has the ability to enforce indictments, it should stop issuing them. Feel-good indictments yield nothing but blood.

CHAPTER 46

I love South Sudan. Its people are long-suffering and resilient, and I admire what they accomplished against what most in the West thought were insurmountable odds. They faced a truly brutal enemy better equipped and larger, and defeated him through enormous sacrifice and perseverance.

But they do have one critical weakness: they have more pride than sense. Through a long and complicated road, it was to be their undoing.

Sudan and South Sudan have constantly teetered on the brink of renewed war. Even though South Sudan is today an independent nation, the border between Sudan and South Sudan remains largely in dispute, and nowhere more so than in the region known as Abyei on the border between Sudan and South Sudan.

The conflict over Abyei has two central causes. The first is that it has oil and Khartoum wants it. South Sudan also wants it, of course. The second is that Abyei is not only a Dinka homeland, but President Kiir and many of the senior members of his government are from Abyei and they have a strong emotional attachment to the land. It's a combination that makes compromise difficult, especially for the political leadership in South Sudan that has suffered at the hands of a northern government that abused, murdered and dislocated so much of the southern population. They are not now inclined to give anything away to Khartoum and it is hard to blame them.

That said, war is a solution that neither side can financially afford, not to mention the loss of life certain to result from renewed conflict.

When the Comprehensive Peace Agreement was signed in 2005, it stipulated two things about Abyei. First, an independent commission would be appointed to determine the exact boundaries of the region, and, second, that a referendum would be held in the province to allow the people residing there to decide whether to be a part of Sudan or South Sudan.

The Abyei Border Commission was composed of fifteen members, five appointed by the government in Khartoum, five by representatives of the south, three by the Intergovernmental Authority on Development, and one each by the United States and Britain. The arbitration was to be final and binding. Essentially, the Commission was supposed to decide what area the Dinka homeland of Abyei included based on historical records of the Dinka chiefdoms in the region.

The Commission presented its report on July 14, 2005, and the government in Khartoum immediately rejected it. Multiple excuses were presented, but the real reason was that the Commission said that Abyei was much larger than Khartoum was willing to accept. Khartoum knew that if a referendum were held, the region would choose to ally itself with the south, and Khartoum would lose all of Abyei's oil fields.

Here, the international community should have put its foot down and said that Khartoum had agreed to binding arbitration and now must accept the outcome. It, however, did not, and a pattern was established that all too often allowed Khartoum to cherry pick what agreements it would hold to and which ones it would not. Khartoum also continued pressuring South Sudan to make concessions, because the West has almost no leverage on Khartoum, but can apply leverage on Juba due to the large amount of foreign aid flowing into the south. It frustrates the government in Juba that they are constantly required to make these concessions while Khartoum regularly thumbs its nose at the West and gets away with it.

The rejection of the arbitration resulted in continuous friction between Sudan and South Sudan along the border, often causing violence. A northern cattle-herding Arab tribe, known as the Messiria, spend part of the year grazing their animals in Abyei. They feared that if Abyei went with the south, they would be blocked from returning. Khartoum provided arms to this tribe and encouraged conflict between the Messiria and the Dinka as a means of weakening the south. Khartoum, of course, denied doing it, but the sophistication of the arms used by the Messiria could only have come from Khartoum, and it was consistent with their past strategy of arming groups to conduct proxy fights of benefit to the regime in Khartoum.

Fighting erupted in 2007 and 2008, causing numerous deaths and the displacement of thousands of southerners.

Following violence in February and March of 2008, the Sudanese government deployed soldiers to Abyei Township on March 31. Fighting broke out between those troops and the southern army in May, resulting in dozens of deaths and the dislocation of about 25,000 to 50,000 mostly Dinka civilians. Khartoum claimed their forces were only reacting to an armed provocation by the south, but with constant friction throughout the province both sides were constantly involved in small-scale fights. Khartoum moved its forces into position and simply acted when they were ready for the assault.

I was part of the team that helped to negotiate an end to the fighting, but the truth was Khartoum had already accomplished its goal of destroying Abyei Township and pushing tens of thousands of Dinka out of the province. It was a form of ethnic cleansing with the goal of reducing the number of Dinka in the hopes that, if a referendum was held, Khartoum had a chance of winning it.

I traveled by U.N. helicopter to Abyei Township after the fighting to inspect the area with American Special Envoy for Sudan, Ambassador Richard Williamson. Parts of the town were still burning and Sudanese forces, to help make it difficult for displaced Dinka civilians to return, had obviously targeted critical infrastructure. To further increase that difficulty of returning, the area had also been heavily mined. The central marketplace was simply gone. Looted possessions stacked by the road were waiting to be picked up in trucks and moved north by Sudanese troops.

The U.N. had an armed peacekeeping base on the outskirts of Abyei Township, yet the U.N. troops did nothing to prevent the fighting or to protect civilians, their primary mission. They simply remained inside their base and watched it happen. It was one of the darkest chapters of the U.N. peacekeeping mission in Sudan. Ambassador Williamson said: "We pay a billion dollars a year for UNMIS and they didn't leave their garrison, while 52,000 lives were shattered and nearly a hundred people perished. The devastation was complete... U.N. peacekeepers and UNMIS staff in their garrison were as close as twenty-five feet away."

I didn't tell my family I was in Abyei. I didn't want them to worry.

CHAPTER 47

One of the strategies that Ambassador Williamson and I developed to try to break the deadlock over the status of Abyei province was to push the north and the south to separate the land and oil issues and negotiate a division of oil resources that Khartoum could live with. Essentially, the south would get the land and the north would get enough of the oil money it needed to sustain the government.

We brought the two sides together, but here is where the south once again showed it had more pride than sense. They refused to negotiate seriously, much to the frustration of Ambassador Williamson, who did his best and was one of the most effective Special Envoys appointed to the job. In 2012, it would also be my honor to work with another outstanding diplomat, Ambassador Princeton Lyman, but that is a later story.

The hatred and distrust between the two sides simply could not be bridged, despite our best efforts. Instead, the south devised a plan to take the issue of Abyei to another round of binding arbitration.

I met several times with Minister to the President Luka Biong Deng, whom I considered a good friend, to try to talk the government out of this approach. Luka was another member of the government whose family was from Abyei, and he was and is a sophisticated and well-educated man.

I pointed out to Luka that President Bashir had already walked away from one round of binding arbitration on Abyei because he didn't like the outcome. By going back to arbitration, the south Sudanese were only giving Bashir another bite at the apple. If it went his way, he would accept it. If it didn't, he would find an excuse to walk away again. It was what he always did.

The solution I pushed with Luka and the government was to sit down and do the hard work of negotiating a political settlement both sides could live with, involving, as I said, the separation of the oil revenue and land issues.

Luka and others in the government were having none of it. Luka was adamant that the Abyei oil was theirs, and that, after all the south had been robbed of and had bled and died for, there was no reason they should offer any compromise on this issue. The oil and the land belonged to the south, and he had confidence that binding arbitration at the international Permanent Court of Arbitration (PCA) in The Hague would find for them. The weight of a decision by such a respected international organization would force Bashir's hand and would produce a result the international community could not allow to be sidestepped.

I disagreed. Yes, it was not right that the south essentially had to buy what rightfully belonged to it by negotiating a land-for-oil deal, but it would give them the land and some of the oil, and as bitter a pill as that was to swallow, it was better in the long run than going back to war, which is what I feared would be the eventual outcome if the two sides did not make a deal.

Luka and the government would not listen to me, and another round of arbitration began. Riek Machar led the arbitration team, with Luka as his co-chair.

On July 22, 2009, the Permanent Court of Arbitration rendered its final decision on the boundaries for Abyei. Essentially, the south lost. Naturally, Bashir immediately embraced the decision.

The judgment redrew the northern, eastern and western boundaries of Aybei, significantly decreasing its size. The redrawn border gave control of the richest oil fields in the region to the north.

The south was boxed in and had little choice but to accept the decision.

The hand of Bashir was greatly strengthened, and although he accepted the decision, he took the oil fields but never implemented the agreement to hold a referendum on the final status of Abyei, with the result that the south did not even get the reduced land area. To this day

Bashir continues to argue over who should be allowed to vote in the referendum (he maintains that the nomadic Northern Misseriya Arabs should be allowed to vote, and until this issue is settled he refuses to hold the referendum), leaving the final status of Abyei in political limbo. The international community has done little to pressure Khartoum to hold the referendum.

Once again, Bashir outfoxed the south. He got everything he wanted and found a means to concede nothing. As I expected.

CHAPTER 48

There were further repercussions to the Permanent Court of Arbitration's ruling. In accepting it, South Sudan made a critical mistake by providing no provisos to their acceptance.

To the east of what had previously been a part of Abyei is an oil-rich sector called Heglig. South Sudan should have said that they accepted the arbitration ruling, but specified that acceptance was not an agreement that Heglig was a part of Sudan rather than South Sudan. There was some reason for this area to remain in dispute, and laying claim immediately would have later strengthened South Sudan's argument. Remaining silent in the face of the ruling appeared to concede the land to the north.

On July 9, 2011, South Sudan officially became the world's newest independent nation. Yet very little of the border between South Sudan and Sudan had been demarked, and Khartoum still asserted ownership of large mineral-rich areas South Sudan considered belonged to it.

To make matters worse, both sides now actively supported rebel movements inside the territory of the other.

Finally, the only oil pipeline available to ship oil out of South Sudan crosses through Sudan. Oil revenue is critical to the survival of both states, but in South Sudan it makes up more than 95% of government revenue.

Naturally, with its pipeline monopoly, Sudan gouged the South in transshipment fees, basically charging in excess of thirty dollars a barrel. Then, on top of that, Khartoum started stealing large amounts of southern oil to divert to its own refineries, and in some cases just outright pocketed the money from the sale of South Sudan's oil.

South Sudan protested, and nothing happened.

Since they were getting less than their fair share of the benefit from the sale of the oil, in frustration South Sudan abruptly shut down the oil fields. Their anger was justified, but once again they acted without serious consideration of the consequences, without a plan for how to deal with those consequences and without consulting their allies. They are among the poorest countries on earth, receiving massive amounts of foreign aid (a large percentage of it from us), and they cut off their primary source of income without a plan while blindsiding their aid donors with the decision. Once again, the government proved itself not ready for prime time.

The donors were furious. In fairness to South Sudan, these same nations showed precious little impatience with Khartoum's shenanigans when pressuring them might have helped the situation, but the bottom line was that South Sudan was now facing economic catastrophe that would ultimately be its undoing.

Now that the government had unilaterally and with almost no warning shut down the oil fields, it slowly began to dawn on them that they needed to create an austerity budget to conserve what limited funds they had left, and they belatedly formed committees to devise financial plans. They invited the donors to participate. I attended many of the meetings, but they were facing a 95% reduction in income and the best of their plans reduced spending by only about 20%, making them unrealistic. I said so repeatedly. It was often acknowledged I was right, but the fantasy plans went forward anyway. There simply was no realistic way to meet the impending financial crisis.

South Sudan put forward a proposal to build an alternative oil pipeline through Kenya or Ethiopia within six months. To even imagine that a pipeline of that magnitude could be constructed safely in that amount of time was delusional. We knew at least two years would be needed in the best of circumstances, and this pipeline had to cross swamps and isolated terrain nearly inaccessible during the rainy season when the primitive dirt roads would be impassible for heavy construction equipment.

The government went to the donors asking us to make up the difference in their financial shortfall. Maybe if, and this is a big maybe, the government had come to us in advance and consulted on a plan for forcing Khartoum to enter into a fair oil deal, with the understanding that should such negotiations fail then the donors would help South Sudan to deal with the situation, then perhaps we might have cooperated. But when the government came to us to ask for additional assistance and a billion-dollar loan (and South Sudan was already one of the largest recipients of U.S. aid in all of Africa), the answer from us was, "No. You got yourself into this mess, you didn't talk to us, and now you'll have to figure it out for yourselves." It was a hard slap of reality. Pride is all well and good, but the southern Sudanese desperately needed to learn some sense.

The move to shut down the oil fields, however, also put enormous economic pressure on Khartoum. There was ample reason for both sides to strike some kind of deal. They both needed the oil income.

Instead the distrust, bitterness and hatred blinded both to reasonable solutions. I had countless arguments with senior members of the South Sudanese government about the need to give up more in oil revenue to the north than they wanted. Yes, it wasn't fair, but war and economic collapse were worse alternatives. The focus of South Sudan needed to be on social, infrastructure and business development, not on a costly pissing match with Khartoum. The problem was that both sides firmly believed the other would implode economically and politically first, and the conflict rapidly devolved into a high stakes game of chicken, further intensified by increased support for rebel movements by each for groups seeking to overthrow the government of the other.

Khartoum still remained the major bad guy in this struggle, continuing to brutalize its own people in Darfur while starting new wars against more of its own people in the states of South Kordofan and Blue Nile in the southern part of their country (states that bordered South Sudan). South Sudan actively supported the rebels.

The failure of South Sudan to act responsibly opened the door for Khartoum to intensify its own campaign to promote ethnic conflict in South Sudan, providing arms to tribes battling each other and to any group opposed to the government in Juba, again sometimes arming both sides in some conflicts. It did not matter to Khartoum who got the guns so long as it hurt South Sudan.

In 2012, Khartoum began bombing places well inside the borders of South Sudan in an attempt to cut off rebel supply lines. Along with our allies, we put pressure on South Sudan not to respond, while very little pressure was placed on Khartoum to stop the attacks. In fairness to us, there was not much pressure we could bring to bear on Khartoum. We already had them under about every kind of sanction available to us.

The Chinese and Russians, who actually have some influence on Khartoum, refused to do much. Chinese companies pump and buy most of the oil from the oil fields in Sudan and South Sudan and, outside of ensuring their continued ability to do that, they showed little interest in engaging Khartoum politically or in using their economic influence to pressure the government.

All over Africa, the Chinese have become a major economic player, but in the worst kind of way. They seek to exploit whatever resources they can, employ a minimum of local labor to do it (preferring to fly in large numbers of even low-level Chinese workers to carry out projects), and show precious little regard for playing a helpful role in the local political scene.

Starting in March of 2012, Khartoum became more aggressive in attacking the border areas of South Sudan, especially out of the area called Heglig.

Also in March of 2012, President Obama called President Kiir to discuss the situation and urge restraint on the part of South Sudan, and Obama thought he had an assurance from Kiir that South Sudan would not resort to military force to resolve its border disputes.

In late March and early April of 2012, fighting along the border in the Heglig area intensified. Because of the remoteness of the region, it is hard to know exactly how events unfolded, but it is certain that Khartoum conducted bombing raids into South Sudan, and it appears Khartoum might have tried to seize some of South Sudan's oil fields near the border.

What is certain is that South Sudan responded militarily, sending their forces into Heglig. Given the economic importance to Khartoum of the oil still being produced there, I expected Sudan to dominate any fighting in order to protect that resource.

Much to my surprise, the southern army kicked ass and drove Sudanese forces into a headlong retreat, with the South occupying the town of Heglig and most of the oil production sites. It was a serious and embarrassing defeat for Khartoum.

South Sudan now found itself with two major problems. First, elements in the Obama Administration were furious with President Kiir's failure to honor his commitment to Obama not to use military force to resolve its border conflicts. Second, the leadership in Khartoum simply could not let this invasion stand, no matter how responsible they were for provoking it. National pride was gravely wounded and they needed the oil fields back. The stability of Bashir's government depended upon it.

This meant we were on the verge of total war along the entire length of the north/south border, a war neither side could afford.

Our ambassador, due to unavoidable circumstances, left the embassy in mid-March and was unable to return until early May, leaving me as the acting ambassador in the middle of a war. I had over 300 frightened local and American employees whose morale I had to carefully manage while carrying a tough message to the senior leadership of the government of South Sudan, many of whom were my friends.

I did get assistance from Special Envoy to Sudan, Ambassador Princeton Lyman, who had replaced Richard Williamson. He flew to Juba to help pressure South Sudan to withdraw its forces from Heglig.

One of the arguments South Sudan now used in defending its action was that Heglig was a territory in dispute, and therefore its status should be up for negotiation. The problem was that they were much too late in making this claim. Having said nothing about Heglig when the second round of arbitration cut it out of Abyei meant South Sudan had appeared to concede the region to Khartoum. Certainly, that was how most people interpreted their stance. It was absolutely true that the ruling made no determination of who owned Heglig, but it was much too late and opportunistic to now be asserting this claim.

As far as we were concerned, it also was not a reason to have invaded militarily when we were promised that territorial claims would be resolved through negotiation.

This all goes back to Special Envoy Richard Williamson's and my attempts to get the two sides to negotiate a political settlement back in 2008. That failure to act meant that South Sudan now laid claim to a much smaller region called Abyei and they had lost the oil fields they could have used as bargaining chips in striking a deal.

Ambassador Lyman and I met with all the movers and shakers in Juba. Our message was tough. Keep your promise not to use military force and withdraw from Heglig or we will sanction you in the United Nations, we will withdraw our economic aid and we will work to get others to do the same.

It was no idle threat, and it shocked the government. They considered us a friend and expected we would support them against the aggression so often inflicted against them by Khartoum.

The problem, as I kept telling them, was that friendship runs two ways. They closed the oil fields without consulting us, and then did not understand our refusal to bail them out. They invaded Heglig when they promised our president they would not, and now they stood on the brink of total war. They refused to take our advice on avoiding a second round of arbitration and had lost. When Kiir met President Obama in New York for a United Nations meeting in 2011, the president asked Kiir not to support rebels fighting the government in Sudan, and Kiir denied any such support. It was a foolish lie because we knew perfectly well aid was flowing across the border. There was even justification for South Sudan aiding those rebel groups (which I will not go into here, but the reasons are compelling) which Kiir could easily have made the case for, but instead he misrepresented what his government was doing with the silly assertion: "What your satellites observe is simply in error."

The inexperience and pigheadedness of the government undermined it at every turn, and vast stores to goodwill on the part of Western governments for South Sudan were foolishly squandered.

Ambassador Lyman, my chief political officer and I visited the office of Pagan Amum, a senior leader of the Sudan People's Liberation Movement at the time, the ruling political party in South Sudan. I have known Pagan for a long time.

Once again we delivered the strong message that, although we were the friends of South Sudan, the government had to withdraw from Heglig for its own good or face a debilitating war that might well destroy the country.

Pagan is an experienced negotiator who had his back to the wall and he knew it. So he pulled out the only card he had left to play, which was to scream what the hell did we care about the future of his country, it was his country and they would decide what was in their best interests.

This is another example of how diplomacy is often theater. I knew perfectly well Pagan was pushing us to see what concessions he could wring out of the United States, and acting belligerent was the only trick he had not tried. I also knew that before the meeting was over we'd all be slapping each other on the back and proclaiming our lasting friendship. This was Pagan's way.

But Ambassador Lyman and my political officer did not know Pagan as well as I did, and Princeton got angry right back at him. That was not a bad strategy to use with Pagan, but hard words were exchanged, and poor Princeton's hands were shaking.

I stepped in and quietly explained to Pagan what I knew he already knew, but that had to be stated anyway so it was out on the table and everyone had a chance to move off the screaming option. I had nothing but respect for South Sudan and its people, I said, but Ambassador Lyman and I were the messengers of Washington. Yes, South Sudan was a sovereign nation that could take whatever action it wished, but Pagan had to understand the consequences. They would be sanctioned in the United Nations, with serious consequences for their economy. Foreign aid would dry up. Western support would evaporate and South Sudan would find itself isolated and alone in facing Khartoum. We were not the creators of these facts, we were the messengers sent by Washington hoping to convince South Sudan to move in a better direction. What South Sudan did in the face of this was up to its leadership to decide.

Princeton confirmed and elaborated on this. Pagan, he said, had to think of the best interests of his people. This military miscalculation would bankrupt the country. They faced total war and a return to the misery of life before the signing of the Comprehensive Peace Agreement. We were their friends and we were speaking to them with a hard message, but a message given in friendship to a people whose future we were deeply concerned for.

By the time we left, everyone was smiling and slapping each other on the back professing our lasting friendship.

I later had a mentoring session with my political officer, explaining what had happened with Pagan and the often theatrical nature of the art of negotiation. Pagan was playing his hand and we had to play ours back. Princeton and I used each other well. Princeton got angry back, I came in as the voice of calm, opening the door for everyone to back off, and Princeton clinched the deal.

South Sudan withdrew from Heglig. Total war was avoided. Thousands of lives were saved.

Sadly, the story of South Sudan did not end there. I left in July of 2012, the day after the celebration of South Sudan's first anniversary of its independence. The mistakes the leadership continued to make were compounding into catastrophe, with little we could do to stop it.

The miscalculation of shutting off the oil, their nearly sole source of revenue, lasted for over a year. The result was that Kiir no longer had the money to support the pigs at the trough he needed in his government to hold together South Sudan's fragile unity. The trade-off of corruption to maintain support collapsed, and Kiir had to make hard choices.

He opted to surround himself with supporters he believed he could count on to back him and tossed out those who opposed him, no matter their tribal connections and importance.

His worst mistake was in July of 2013, when he tossed Riek Machar out of the government and appointed a new vice president.

The outcome was all too predictable. Machar formed an opposition movement to Kiir and in December of 2013 fighting broke out, essentially tribally based.

Kiir claims Machar staged a coup. I doubt that. What I think happened is that there was an attempt to disarm elements in the army loyal to Machar (who were, for the most part, Nuer tribesmen) because Kiir feared a possible coup. The soldiers refused to disarm and fought back. It was a bad miscalculation on the part of Kiir, and the house of cards that is South Sudan came tumbling down.

Today the country is tearing itself apart in a civil war between competing ethnic groups. All of the goodwill South Sudan had accumulated with the West has been squandered and the donors have largely washed their hands of the country.

Machar and Kiir both have much to answer for in this. Kiir, having been in power since 2005, should have announced that he would not stand for reelection and set a precedent for the peaceful change of leadership, as George Washington did in our country. Instead, he is turning into yet another African strongman.

Machar has no chance of becoming the president of South Sudan. Why he persists in this delusion is incomprehensible to me. This is even truer today now that he leads a rebel army against the government he once served. He will never gain international recognition, even in the unlikely event that his rebel army succeeds in toppling the government.

Instead of working for the good of their country, the national leadership is tearing itself and the nation apart in a spiraling cycle of hate, ambition, death, destruction and poverty. Having ignited intertribal violence in support of a foolish and self-serving quest for individual political power and ambition, the leadership has lost control of the violence and intertribal war burns on with little hope or means for extinguishing it. Given the obstinacy of Kiir's and Machar's determination to hang on to or seize power at any cost to the country they should be serving, I see no way out.

The people of South Sudan deserve better. We did our best to try and help; their leaders were determined not to listen.

It is a powerful lesson our own political leadership should heed. The extreme polarization and tribalization of our political life and institutions is the greatest threat to our democracy since our own Civil War killed 625,000 Americans. We now face a cold Civil War in America. Our democracy might not survive it.

CHAPTER 49

In late September of 2012, I retired and left a life of diplomatic work after over twenty-three years of service.

On the occasion of my father's eightieth birthday, I wrote him the following letter.

Dear Dad,

I had a great time visiting last weekend. Although I know the double bypass surgery was no walk in the park, believe me when I say that you look better. In a few months, I am sure you are going to feel better than you have in years.

Like that 80th birthday button you received as a gift that said, "After 80 years, I've survived just about everything," in 80 years of living you have seen and done much, most of it dedicated to the service of our country.

You were 17 when you joined the army to fight in World War II, one of the few wars worth fighting. You were training for the invasion of Japan when the war ended, an invasion everyone knew would result in enormous casualties on both sides. Fortunately for me, the war finished before that invasion, but you stood ready to do your part no matter the cost.

You later joined the United States Agency for International Development and you spent the rest of your working life serving your country overseas doing your best to lift people in foreign societies out of crushing poverty. In my mind, it has always been the generosity of the American people, their willingness to reach out to others to help those in need, that has most honorably distinguished the spirit of our country. USAID was not always managed well, and was sometimes used for political ends instead of to help people, but never by you, Dad. You were the human face of that program, working tirelessly on behalf of others. You spent your life working for your family, your country, and your world. Your commitment and compassion have always been my inspiration, and the model for how I have tried to live my own life. More than that, I was always loved and taken care of, and I have always known that. I love you very much, and I am proud of who you are and what you have done.

More than Green Lantern, my parents were my moral compass, my real heroes. My mother was also an extraordinary woman, kind, smart and loving, who worked hard taking a leadership role in many organizations that gave back to her community. The best thing that ever happened to me was that I was the son of these two remarkable people who always gave more than they took.

Dad passed on July 10, 2014 and Mom on September 16, 2017.

In Oklahoma there is a monument to people like my parents, and, I think, a monument to me and to all those who have dedicated their lives to their fellow men and women in the hope of making the world a better place while trying to represent the best of the American spirit. It is called public service, the commitment to do your all for the country that has given us so much, a desire to strengthen the heart of the nation and to try to add something, no matter how small, to its great heritage and to the future generations of Americans who will follow us.

This memorial is on the ground of what used to be the Alfred E. Murrow building in Oklahoma City.

The people we elect to represent us in Washington all too often gratuitously trash public servants, call them parasites and heartless bureaucrats, forgetting that if there is red tape in government, and if public servants have to sometimes do things that anger the average man or woman, we do it because we must carry out the very laws that those elected officials have placed on us. The American public, you and me, elect these people, and public servants are sworn to uphold the laws they fashion. This is how democracy works, the very thing that I have passionately defended around the world and even risked my life for, just as my father did before me.

For our political leadership, it is easy to blame government workers for how the government operates and what it does. And so we are labeled bureaucrats, or the deep state, as though we made the laws and created the system we work so hard to serve.

We are called bureaucrats, that is, until we make the ultimate sacrifice in the line of duty, just as those 168 government workers did in the Murrow building in 1995 in Oklahoma City. On that day, those men, women, and nineteen of their children stopped being bureaucrats and the nation honored them as public servants who gave their lives for their country. They were not killed by Osama bin Laden or any foreign madman, but by one of our own countrymen, a twisted man who hated his own government. He forgot that in America, when you stab at the government and those who serve it, perhaps imperfectly but with dedication, you stab at the heart of our national soul, our nation itself. We are a democracy and, whether we like it or not, when we look at our government, we look into a mirror. We own both the perfections and the imperfections.

At the memorial in Oklahoma City are 168 empty chairs, nineteen of them smaller for the children who died. Each stands waiting silently for an occupant who will never return.

These were people who stood by an oath that might well have been:

In brightest day,
In blackest night,
No evil shall escape my sight.
Let those who worship evil's might,
Beware my power,
Green Lantern's Light.

I am proud to have stood with them.

95647669R00120

Made in the USA
Columbia, SC
20 May 2018